Kimberly Smith embodies honesty and authenticity in the depth of who she is. In this beautifully raw and very rich book, Kimberly brings her truest self to the pages she has penned. You will stand on the landscape of her life with tears and with validation for your own hurts and disappointments. Her story encompasses deep valleys of great pain, but even greater revelation of Living Hope. Kimberly is an overcomer and a victor, and her life bears the redemption of every single story in this book. This is a gem of incredible practicality, reflection and transparency, and if you will take her hand, she will walk you to your own personal victory. That's the hope for this book. It's not an easy road but grab another Sister and traverse these pages together, it will be worth it!

Julie King is the Director of Arise through East West Ministries. She is a wife and mom of four courageous daughters. She is a passionate lover of Jesus and passionate about the world He died for. Her heart for revival compels her to lead women around the world to take the gospel to those who have never heard the precious name of Jesus. She is also the author of her first book, "Arise My Darling."

Whether you are all put together or falling to pieces, *Beautifully Broken* is a must read. In person, Kim lights up a room, makes you feel valuable, and will wildly share her faith in Jesus with you. This book is a permanent document that can be revisited anytime you need to be reminded that *you are enough*, it is *okay* to fall apart and not have it all together, and *God loves you*. By the way, so does Kim. She finds Jesus in everyone she meets. Whether in person or in written word, Kim offers encouragement, transparency, good humor and thought provoking questions to help lead to restoration. This is not a self-help book; this is a manual for a life well lived. I thank and congratulate my dear friend Kim for her passion and willingness to expose the truth to help others in her book, *Beautifully Broken*.

Julie Davenport, Wife, Mother, Community Activist, and Entrepreneur

When I first met Kim, it was love at first sight. I imagine she gets that a lot. She is beautiful from the inside out, a true reflection of Christ. As I listened to her story, I recognized someone who has experienced trauma and used it to advance her faith walk. Kim's story will touch the heart of every woman, regardless of their age or station in life. She is an encourager, an overcomer, and a cheerleader for God's gals to rise from the ashes and live to the full. Grab a pen and dig in to the deep-dive questions and lessons at the end of each chapter. You will be blessed.

Mary Ethel Eckard, Author, Speaker, and Co-Founder of Dragonfly Ministries

Wow! The stories Kim shares here are so raw and real…. Yet full of grace and hope at the same time. Kim's ability to witness her own journey from the perspective of God's love is reaffirming to me; makes me look at my own journey in a whole new way. This book will be a bible of sorts for other women, who are navigating murky waters and living in messy times right now. This book will help them find their way back to center and back to what's true and pure about who they really are. I highly recommend it.

April Adams Pertuis, Storytelling Expert, Visibility Strategist. Founder of the LIGHTbeamers Community

BEAUTIFULLY BROKEN

FORGED THROUGH FIRE, UP FROM ASHES

Kimberly Smith

Beautifully Broken
Forged through Fire, Up from Ashes

Kimberly Smith

To contact the author:
kim@beautifullybrokenx3.com
www.beautifullybrokenx3.com

The sunflower on the cover is a reminder of how God loves our children even more than we do. We can trust them in His care. They are in His grip. We don't have to worry about their future because God has a plan for them. Just as the sunflower tends to reposition itself to face the sun, just as it can tolerate heat and draught, our role as moms is to constantly point our children to Jesus, even during their times of wilderness, knowing He will keep them in His grip. Because, again, He loves them far more than we do.

Published by:

Mary Ethel

Mary Ethel Eckard
Frisco, Texas

ISBN (Print): 978-1-7357853-0-1
ISBN (E-book): 978-1-7357853-1-8

Dedication

Dedicated to my first love, Jesus. Thank you
for making this book possible.

Kyle, Haleigh, Anna, Luke, and Preston
I love you more than life itself and can't imagine spending
the final chapters of my life with anyone else.

Special Thanks

To Kyle, thank you for loving me for who I am. Thank you for grounding me when the world starts spinning. Thank you for making me laugh countless times a day. I'm certain you're adding years to my life. I'm also certain the best is yet to come and cannot wait to be out in those wide-open spaces we dream about. Your love heals me. You are my best friend and the love of my life. I truly adore you.

To my girls, Haleigh and Anna, where do I begin? You are so much of the reason for this book. You have been my inspiration, my motivation, and my reason for over 26 years. I wouldn't trade one day of our journey, even those in the fire. Watching you now, rise from the ashes and become the beautiful, smart, incredible women God created you to be is a gift. I will forever love you more.

To my boys, Luke and Preston, it is an outright blast raising you two boys. I fall more in love with you every day. You, along with your sisters, are my reason and my motivation. You are brave and kind. You are fun and adventurous. You're more than I could ever ask for in a son, and I cannot wait to see what God has planned for your lives. I like you as much as I love you!

To my Mom, thank you for being my Ruth, the one who takes my urgent 3 a.m. calls and comes running. The one who has been there for every single heartbreak. The one who checks on me when I'm struggling. The one who comes over to hold me while I cry. I cannot imagine my life without you. Thank you for loving me unconditionally, for being my biggest fan and cheerleader, for being a "mean mom" when it counted. You showed me strength and dignity. I love you beyond words.

To my beautifully, blended family - Dad, thank you for a lifetime of unconditional love. It held me together. Daddy-Keith, thank you for loving me like your own. I am who I am because of that. Eric, I adore you and wouldn't want to have walked this crazy journey with anyone else. You're forever my hero. Annie, thank you for being bold and fun and fierce, for being my friend when I needed one. Stephanie, oh the secrets you have kept. My partner in crime, my sister, and at times my voice of reason. Jami, little sister, you bring true joy and laughter into my life. I have loved watching you grow into an amazing woman. Jade, my baby sister. I have loved you from the moment you came into this world, and like your mom, you are a force to be reckoned with. Kathryn, my sister-in-love, you inspire me and crack me up all at the same time. Thank you for loving Eric well. Erin Paige, there aren't words for the gift you became when you entered my life. I love watching you grow into the beautiful woman God created you to be. My brothers-in-love, sister-in-love, nieces and nephews, aunts and uncles, cousins - thank you for the craziness, the fun, and the sweet love you provide that makes life worth living.

My Tribe - Kari, Jamie, Jamie, Amy, Tiffany, Nicole, Jessica, Julie, Julie, Ingrid, Kristen, and Sandy, you are and have been the best girlfriends and soul sisters a girl could ever want. Thank you for cheering me on, for supporting my dreams, for calling me out, for praying for me and my family. I truly don't know what I would do without you. Your friendship has meant everything to me. I love and appreciate you. (Jeff, I can't help but include you in my tribe. Best guy friend a girl could have.)

Journey to Dream Team, you turned my life all kinds of upside down in only the best of ways. Watching you love like Jesus and serve others was one of the best experiences of my life. I will forever consider you sons and daughters, friends, and will always love you much.

Mary and April, what an unbelievable gift you are. Thank you for your belief in me. Thank you for making this book and its launch what it is. Thank you for seeing things in me I often can't see. You inspire and motivate me, and I am blessed by your gifts and talent. Thank you for the countless beautifully broken women you help through Dragonfly Ministries and LIGHTbeamers.

Precious reader, I am beyond honored you picked up or bought this book. Your story is the inspiration behind it. We all find ourselves broken. We all spend time in the pit. AND, we all have what it takes to make an unbelievable comeback. I have prayed for you and your future. Let your journey of grace and overcoming, of freedom and joy, start now. You are so worth it. (You'll hear that a lot!)

Contents

Foreword

Hello Sweet Sister,

We've been anxiously waiting to meet you.

Whether you realize it today, tomorrow, or somewhere in-between the pages that follow, you are now a part of the family. Please believe us when we tell you, we could not be more thankful and excited about that. Welcome to the journey, beautiful.

I guess we should start by proudly letting you know that the amazing woman writing this book is our Mama. Kimberly "Superwoman" Smith. Defeater of all irrational fears, healer of all heartbreaks, protector against all thieves of joy. Master of comfort and reassurance. I think you get the point – she's a very, very big deal around here.

With all those titles you would think she would be ready to hang up her cape and retire after 26 years, right? We have wondered our entire lives, "How on Earth does she do it?" and "God, does this woman ever get tired?" only to find out time and time again, she's just getting started.

As little girls, our mom did everything she could to protect everything we were that maybe the world thought we shouldn't be. She wanted our spirits wild, our imaginations limitless, and our self-acceptance strong. Now that we are adults, she stands on the sidelines. Our ultimate cheerleader and best friend. Waiting and ready at any moment to remind us that failure is okay, redemption is real, and mistakes are expected.

A real life angel, right? We know. We got really lucky, sis.

Time to address the elephant in the room.

It is very possible these words feel like salt in a wound. Maybe your chest feels heavy right about now. Maybe reading about our super-present super-mom is stirring up emotions you thought you left behind long ago. Maybe you've rolled your eyes a few times. Maybe it isn't even a mom-issue, it's a dad-issue. Whatever it is, please feel it, and thank you for getting this far. You will soon find out that we understand. We have been there. A few times.

Our greatest hope is that in this book, you begin to heal. Parts of Mom's story may feel terrifying to sit with and that is okay. That means it's working. HE is working.

Yes, here comes the Jesus piece.

It is safe to say neither of us are strangers to struggle. Our laundry list of trauma and damage we still need to work out gets longer every single day. Although we claimed to be followers of Christ most of our lives, we trudged. There have been many dark and hazy nights where we absolutely rocked our mother's world with fear. We can honestly say there were many days she thought she would lose one of us to our own devices.

What does that feel like now? Shameful. I mean when we are in this constant cycle and life of insanity, we don't see the damage we could be causing to others along the way. So, when we both got real with ourselves and accepted help, we were faced with the constant self-defeating thought of… "Are we broken?"

Thankfully, at a very young age, our Mom taught us about the unconditional love of Jesus. How lucky were we? To not only know the unconditional love of her, but to know the unconditional love of Jesus.

He answered our questions loud and clear.

"To be broken is its own kind of beautiful." Just because we are broken does not mean we are unable to be loved, adored or cherished. By our mothers, our fathers, our sisters and our brothers, we are loved.

The most unimaginable pain, brokenness, and hurt can be healed by Him. Believe us when we say that.

As your read this, we pray you are overcome with peace and hope. That you feel our mama's love and hear her words. Wherever you resonate, we are with you.

Again, we are so thankful you are here. We love you and believe you are right where you are supposed to be. We are honored to have a mother like ours. Not only to spread love and understanding, but to leave the enormous impact on you that she will forever leave on us.

Haleigh and Anna
Daughters of Superwoman

How to Use This Book

"It's not the size of the girl in the fight. It's the size of the fight in the girl."

In her book, "Beautifully Broken," Kim vulnerably, honestly, and tenderly shares her life story of growing up in the midst of trauma and how those unhealed emotions and fears guided her down many wrong paths in the first half of her life. She offers sound self-help to the reader as she shares her own pain and healing, holding the hand of the reader to walk through their personal pain.

At the end of each chapter, Kim includes "Lessons Learned" and "Questions to Consider." To get the most from this book, steal away to a quiet place, dig deep within your spirit, and find your answers. Journal your thoughts and prayers as you work through each chapter. Write in the margins, underline, circle and highlight words or phrases that resonate with you. You will be amazed at the inner change that comes as you sit in the quiet, reflecting on your life, and journaling your thoughts, emotions, wounds, and need for wholeness.

Work through these chapters at your pace. Open your heart, mind, spirit, and emotions as you read. Put yourself within the story – feel the pain, savor the advice and the compassion, celebrate the victories, and allow healing to wash over you. Revisit places from your past.

Revisit them physically, if possible, to help you recover the pieces that have been shattered. Revisit them emotionally and allow the gift of time and wisdom to provide insight and healing. Revisit them spiritually and picture Jesus with you amid every detail, giving love and support.

Intentionally journey through these pages by taking your brokenness to new heights; use the scars and pain from the fires of your past to forge the shattered pieces into a heart healed by the touch of God. You, too, will be able to say, "I am no longer shattered, for I was broken and now I'm beautifully healed, forged through fire."

Be assured! Your spiritual healing, paired with your emotional and physical healing, will bring life in abundance!

Mary Ethel Eckard
Dragonfly Ministries

Introduction

Forty-plus trips around the sun. I had lived half a lifetime when my "undoing" took place. And by undoing, I mean shattering. S-H-A-T-T-E-R-I-N-G. There's not enough emphasis I can put on that word, even if that one word filled this entire page in giant, red, bold, italic, underlined letters. It was a shattering of my heart, soul, mind, and spirit; the type of undoing you think you may never recover from.

My guess is you have experienced your own season of shattering, or you wouldn't be reading this book. If you're in that place right now, *Beloved*, I am *so* sorry. What I would give to sit with you, both of us with a cup of coffee or a glass of wine, sharing our stories, encouraging you, convincing you, "You *will* make it through this."

You will.

I think that's what I want you to take away most from this book, the motivation and belief that you have what it takes. That no matter what season you're in, there is still good to chase. Quitting is not the answer. Keep fighting. Keep going. Believe that you can.

Because you can.

This planet is hard on hearts, isn't it? Brutal, I think. I've learned, on this crazy journey called life, that sometimes it's in our deepest suffering we find our true selves. It's where we find the grace and grit to keep going. It's often where we find God. In the pages of this book, I share in all transparency my highs and lows, my colossal mistakes, my heartbreaks, and even the fires I've walked through (and sometimes sat in), allowing God to shape me into the woman I am today. And please hear me when I say, I am not "there" yet. Wherever "there" is. I am so far from perfect. Completely flawed. Completely human. But I am also proof there is joy on the other side of pain. There is healing in and through our journey, even when we don't understand it, *if* we allow it.

Growing up, most of us believe our lives are relatively "normal." Others may see our life a bit more colorful than theirs, by comparison, but what we grow up in and around indeed becomes our norm. Right or wrong, our surroundings are "the house" that builds us.

I believe we all experience some level of dysfunction. Many are blessed to grow up with very little trauma, or even drama, so to speak. Others feel cursed by the never-ending feeling that the other shoe is about to drop. Children are resilient and often oblivious to the kind of evil that shatters families, hearts and lives. Those same children are often forced to normalize (or conform) simply to survive.

Like most, I didn't grow up a stranger to heartbreak. My little girl heart, like many of yours, was bruised and scarred by divorce, betrayal, abuse, and more. The need for approval, among other things, impacted choices and decisions that played a major role in creating chaos and drama throughout much of my life. Without knowing why, I seemed to always end up right back in the forger's fire.

At least, that is, until my season of shattering hit. It felt like a hurricane that wouldn't pass. It was like the eye of the storm was stuck over our home. Wave after wave, day after day, pure exhaustion. The reality is, I'm not one to quickly become undone. I'm a survivor by nature. An overcomer. Resilient. But this time was different, I struggled to bounce back. My undoing had come, and it felt like the broken pieces of my life couldn't be put back together. I had no idea how to hold myself together, much less put myself back together.

It didn't take long to realize this brokenness was cyclical. The pattern was not just painfully familiar, it was destroying me. I had to break the cycle and stop the return of another tsunami. I had to figure out my role in stirring up the storm. Realizing I was part of the problem helped me understand I could also be part of the healing.

I began to realize I had spent years seeking applause and approval, becoming who and what others wanted me to become, maybe even who and what I thought the world wanted me to become. I wore the hats of career woman, social butterfly, country club girl, and pastor's wife, to name a few.

But, this shattering started me on a journey of recovery. Recovery I had embarked on repeatedly for years prior, but never fully embraced. The question: "Who am I?" *really* haunted me. Yes, I am a survivor, an overcomer; I am resilient. God gave me those qualities. But there had to be more. There had to be more required to stop the cycle of insanity I was in.

I imagine you, too, are a survivor, an overcomer, resilient. You may not feel that way right now. There's a chance you may wonder if you'll ever feel normal again, if you'll find peace and purpose in or through the pain. You will.

Each of our stories are filled with brokenness - some caused by us, some done to us. We have the opportunity to make the best of our brokenness and redirect our stories. To find our happy ending. To find our true selves. They're both inside jobs—being happy and figuring out what makes us tick. Finding myself meant embracing the fact that I don't belong in an office or board room in heels. I'm somewhere in the middle of being a conservative and a liberal. I believe in Jesus and love my gay friends. I dream of living in the country with horses and dogs, and I'm happiest when I'm with my husband and our four kids.

All of these realizations (and a few more) came out of suffering. Actually, they came out of healing from suffering.

**Had it not been for the fire,
I would never have discovered the woman
God created me to be.**

And do you know what? I like me. And girls, that's saying a lot. There's a verse in the Bible that pretty much sums up my story. "What the enemy meant for harm, God used for good."[1] I am a walking, talking testament of that!

What about you? Do you like who you are? Are you striving endlessly to be who the world tells you to be? Have you invested the time in finding your true self?

There's so much I pray you get from my story. I'm honored you're here. I hope you see God's grace and mercy, not just in my story but also in yours. I hope you believe that you matter, that you are **_enough_**, exactly the way God made you. I hope you know that you, too, have a powerful comeback story.

Here's to bravely stepping into the women and the warriors God created us to be. *Beautifully broken. Forged through fire.*

Up from the ashes.

CHAPTER ONE

The Writing on the Wall

"She is what the world loves to hate – pure, authentic, tested, and brave. And that is why her kind will save the world."

JOHNNY NGUYEN

efore jumping headfirst into my story, I should probably preface it by giving you a bird's eye view of my personality. Understanding the way God wired me may help you relate better to my method of writing, or even to my story. So, the "overcomer, resilient, survivor" gene I talk about comes from my mom. I don't wallow or sit in pain well, and I hate anything that remotely looks or sounds like a pity-party. Some say I'm "too positive." Others call it "peppy."

My beloved firstborn, Haleigh, voiced at an early age that she would never be a cheerleader. Offended and in my most cheerleader, peppy voice I asked, "Why not?" Her answer was simple and felt a bit harsh for a first grader, "Because I don't want to be peppy like you." I laughed. I owned it and so began our relationship based on complete acceptance and unconditional love.

Peppy also means I have a good deal of energy and get excited easily. I'm prone to drama. At times, I come off as "too passionate." I grew up seeing the best in everyone around me, which at times, proved to be detrimental and frustrated my mom to no end. I was always pulling for the underdog, feeling the need to fight for social injustice, or standing up for *the least of these.*

I'm blunt and transparent. My life and words come without a filter. I am crazy in love with Jesus, and love talking about Him. He is *everything* to me. I am far from a saint. More like a redeemed mess, thus Beautifully Broken. I know my need for forgiveness – and grace. Notice I said that in present and not past tense.

I'm a dreamer (I prefer the word visionary). My dreams are mostly outrageous and sometimes involve a level of disappointment. Don't believe me? Keep reading.

The tale of Cinderella is my favorite. For the first half of my life, I wholeheartedly believed my prince was on his way. However, as one of my mentors put it, life taught me there were far too many frogs to kiss and shoes to try on. It taught me wicked women really do exist and clearly, my fairy godmother lost or forgot my address.

It's hard to find a prince when you're attracted to bad boys. Sure I believed it was love - *every* time. My love just looked like a lot of fixing and saving. My *need* to fix or save others was something that tripped me up for years, bringing pain into not only my little girl heart but much of my adult life.

In case you haven't seen it yet, there's a bit of a martyr in me. Oh, how I loved hearing, "you've changed him" or "you make me a better person." Ughhhh… I also struggle with codependency and ego, both foundational pieces that led to my repeated brokenness.

From a positive and peppy perspective,
you can't surrender to God
what you don't know needs to be healed.

Anyway, back to my undoing.

My First Two Marriages. (Please don't judge.)

Let's talk about my first marriage. Briefly. I met my first husband when we were in college. Our marriage produced two amazing, beautiful daughters, Haleigh and Anna, who were and have always been *my life*. The marriage ended as a result of unfaithfulness. When I found out, I was heartbroken. But with two little girls to provide for, I jumped into the roles of single mom and career woman without doing the work required to see my part in our broken marriage.

My single mom years were some of the best years of my life, despite the challenges that come from raising children as a party of one. We were involved in a wonderful church and had a terrific circle of friends. I was looking for answers (aka healing). I was even looking to God for those answers. About nine years into single-motherhood, I wanted a partner. I had always wanted to be a wife. I believed in the happily-ever-after, and I wanted a healthy family and a strong home for my daughters.

In 2006, when my girls were ages twelve and nine, I met and married a man I was sure, before we even met face to face, was God-sent. We met online. He was a pastor, nonetheless; and because of my tendency to dream big, I *just knew* he was the holy man that would right every wrong from my past (a ridiculously tall order). I also *knew* he would provide stability and the perfect home my kids deserved. Plus, he had a beautiful daughter close in age to my girls whom I fell in love with. My fairy tale mentality assured me we would be the blended family that lived happily ever after.

Our marriage was anything but stable from the get-go, as would be expected after dating four short months. Because we were having sex outside of marriage, I feared we wouldn't have God's blessing, so we fast tracked our marriage. I can still see the deer-in-the-headlight look our daughters had during the ceremony. *God bless them.* We truly thought we were doing what was best for them.

We were all a bit disillusioned from the beginning. While I was convinced this pastor had to be perfect in leading our family, he too expected something different from a "godly wife." The truth is, demons and old habits surfaced immediately. It was hard, and we both wondered what we had done. In a matter of months, the exact circumstance that destroyed my first marriage seemed to be threatening my second.

Certain *it* was rearing its ugly head, the detective in me kicked in. My past life and experiences had allowed me to become quite crafty at playing Sherlock Holmes. I joke, but it felt tragically familiar. Painfully familiar. I knew to check phone records, and just like before, I demanded them. The result was the same, fears confirmed. It was horribly cruel, I thought.

Surely, God wouldn't put me through the same devastation again. I mean, did He not know this was more than I could bear? How much did He expect one woman to take? I remember distinctly being on our bedroom floor that morning, on my knees, sobbing. Asking God why. How could He allow the same pain, again? He could have stopped it or prevented it. But, He didn't, and I didn't understand.

We hadn't even been married a year. In shock, my instinct was to deny the seriousness of it. I reasoned that Satan was trying to destroy what God had planned. I mean, an emotional affair doesn't carry the same weight, right? I told myself it shouldn't bear the same consequence. After all, I wasn't prepared to walk through that kind of heartache again, and I certainly wasn't interested in the humiliation another broken marriage would bring. I couldn't fathom telling my family or friends. I couldn't imagine telling our daughters.

So, wearing my rose-colored glasses, I convinced myself this emotional entanglement wasn't the same as a physical affair, that I could rebound, and I resolved to fix and save our marriage. After all, that's what I did – I "fixed and saved." I resolved to be a better wife, to change my behavior, which would convict him to change his ways.

I didn't question God at this point. Like a "good" Christian, I assumed God would use this situation to make us stronger. But doubt and lack of trust are massive, heavy weights for a new marriage. Too heavy. Every behavior, word, and tone I observed in him were under scrutiny. I was constantly on alert. Questions and insecurities swirled in my mind - Will he be attracted to the new girl at work? Did he really have to stay late for a meeting? His voice sounds off. He didn't say "I love you" before ending the call.

Everything was questioned and my insecurities surfaced and camped out on the edge of my nerves.

Anyway, we struggled through our first few years of marriage. The doubting and questioning were a burden for both of us. But we did life together. We had fun, wonderful times as a couple and as a family. We became pregnant with a beautiful little boy we named Luke. Living with a new baby and three teenage girls kept us busy. On top of all that, we ran a ministry together that we loved.

Happily Never After

But unlike the fairy tale ending we were hoping for, we found ourselves back in the same place a few years later. Infidelity raised its ugly head, and this time it was more than an emotional affair. This time, it made less sense. The "other woman" wasn't his type. She definitely was not the "godly woman" he said he wanted. He had sold me on that when we were dating. She was his assistant at work, and while my gut told me for months there was an attraction on her part, I continued to tell myself he wouldn't risk our marriage.

Nonetheless, there it was, in black and white. There was no denying it. You'd think the discovery process and realizing your gut was right would bring some kind of satisfaction. It doesn't. The shock and disbelief is still crippling. I felt like I had been punched in the gut. Like I couldn't breathe. Hot tears silently streamed down my face as I read the emails. How long had they been seeing each other? Was he in love with her?

A million questions and thoughts swirled through my mind. The question I longed for a man to answer had been answered. Again. I was unworthy of love. At least not the faithful, committed, forever kind of love I desperately wanted. Through his actions, I was reminded of the fear that drove my need. My need to know I wasn't worthless, unlovable. I wasn't too much.

It felt as if a bomb went off inside my chest. My heart shattered. Nothing was sacred. Nothing felt safe. Our marriage vows became meaningless. The bed and the house, his words, everything felt hollow. The rose-colored glasses were removed and I could see clearly the things I tried for so long to justify and deny.

Even when the writing is on the wall, we may choose not to see it. Maybe childhood trauma taught us, far too early in life, that denial is a better way to survive. Rose-colored glasses keep children from seeing evil they're too young to understand – or feel. For some of us, those rose-colored glasses are a necessity in our wardrobe, even as we grow older. We go nowhere without them because we can't take the risk of feeling the pain that comes in seeing the truth.

And thus began years of unraveling. Our daughters, all three of them, began to spiral out of control in different ways. The ministry we loved felt impossible. I was exhausted and scared. My body hurt all over as a deep depression set in. I could sleep for days, but never at night - wide awake, with my thoughts and questions. I looked like I felt. **Shattered.**

The shock lingered. I couldn't believe infidelity happened again. Honestly, I couldn't believe God allowed it. I had been obedient to what I believed God was calling me to do. I had served. I had changed. Transformed by Jesus, as they say. Leaving a sinful past to be in full-time ministry. I was also committed to this marriage, the raising of our daughters and our young son. When I dove in, I was *all in!*

To get a better understanding, we should backtrack a few years. My past life was unquestionably a train wreck full of bad choices. But after my first divorce, I decided to try the "God-thing." That's what I mean by *all in*. God seemed to be the answer to having a happy family. God-honoring families stayed together. Maybe if I invited God into our family, *this* would work for my girls and me.

In my naivety, I believed surrendering my life to God would equal *blessings* and by blessings, I mean favor. God's favor. The white-picket-fence type favor. The kind where my daughters would never know the pain I had. I believed that somehow, God would shield them from the ugliness of the world, and they would grow up to move on to their own white-picket-fences. But *this* was not a *blessing. This* felt far from favor. *This* was a nightmare, another storm I had no power to control, another disaster I was dragging my innocent children through. Remember I told you many of my dreams were accompanied by disappointment. This white-picket-fence favor was no exception. The dream exploded. My best attempts to earn or win or manipulate God's favor were in vain.

The Hard Work Begins

Instead of feeling blessed, I had to face the truth that, again, I wasn't chosen. Someone had been chosen over me. I had to sit in pain that felt unbearably familiar.

All my life, I wanted to be chosen. Chosen for cheerleader. Chosen for homecoming queen or any other award that meant value. Value as in popular. Then I wanted to be chosen over drugs, over alcohol. Chosen over "her" – whoever she was. In my heart, chosen equaled love. But in my state of need, chosen also meant chasing, and my years of chasing were leaving me dimmer and dimmer, a shell of the woman I wanted to be. As long as I was chasing being chosen, the lies from the enemy couldn't catch me. But now, in my pain, I succumbed to the lies that forever chased me. "I'm not lovable." "I'm not enough." "Maybe I'm too much."

This time when betrayal hit, I had come a long way in my faith and walk with Jesus. I had Him to lean on, but I also had questions only He could answer. I think the thing that shattered me the most after this affair was questioning God's heart for me. Somehow in my mind I believed my obedience to Him would shield me from evil and pain, and yet I felt more exposed and more heartbroken than I had ever experienced.

So, with the obvious cycle being infidelity, I went back to dissect my first divorce, hoping to find answers. It was different, but the betrayal felt the same. The messages or untruths were repeated. "You're not pretty enough, sexy enough, fun enough, etc." The difference is that my first husband and I were young and college sweethearts. Okay, that's a bit of a stretch. We hooked up and dated our last semester of college; everyone was getting married, and it seemed like the best next step, so why not?

Why not? WHY NOT?

Because, we both had a lifetime of baggage to process. However, without any concept of "baggage," in we jumped. Headfirst into marriage, bringing the worst version of our selves without understanding why. Before you set out to ride into the sunset with your prince, know your stuff. Know your baggage. Unpack your baggage. We all have it. Heal what needs to be healed. You're worth it. Your future relationships are worth it.

The truth is we attract those who are at the same place we are in our emotional wellbeing and maturity. Meaning, when we carry our fair amount of baggage, we will meet a man with just as much baggage. Baggage begets baggage, and too many of us don't get the help we need to unpack it. Therefore, we tend to re-live patterns that are self-defeating and not good for us. Worse, we pass it on to our children.

Sometimes these patterns are born from trauma. Wikipedia defines trauma as: damage to the mind that occurs as a result of a distressing event, often the result of an overwhelming amount of stress that exceeds one's ability to cope or integrate the emotions involved with that experience.

The best way I've heard trauma explained is from a drug and alcohol counselor who said trauma occurs when our world no longer feels safe in an overwhelming way. Trauma looks like the little boy afraid to go home after school because of the violence that ensues for no apparent reason. Trauma may look like the woman who was raped and now sleeps with the lights on. Trauma can come from a car accident, a death, an illness.

Most of us understand trauma as it relates to war and those who serve our country. The day in and day out horror of bombings and death, the experiences that overwhelm a soldiers' systems and ability to process all they hear and see. But trauma isn't limited to the military. Its effects are widespread.

Trauma is more common than we think. It also changes us.

Beautiful One, it's important you know that God didn't strike me down in my questioning, my doubt, or even in my anger. He didn't turn away when I screamed at Him, wanting to know why. He moved in closer. He sat with me in my pain, only asking for my honesty. He knows our hearts anyway. He knows the magnitude of our pain and our endless questions. He wants to take us on a journey of healing and restoration. He can remove those rose-colored glasses once and for all, so we can see the truth – the whole truth – and head toward lasting recovery. Don't get stuck in the mire or in playing detective. What others choose to do to us is just that, their choice. We can't control or stop their bad decision despite our best efforts. But we can take care of ourselves. We can allow God to love us back to life. We must. If you're overcoming infidelity or some other tragedy, God is ready to meet you where you are. To start your comeback story. Maybe this is the first page of a brand-new chapter.

LESSONS LEARNED

The odds are you have experienced trauma in one form or another. We are wise to acknowledge its fallout and to accept the healing we deserve. Recognizing events from childhood, or even as adults, that could have caused trauma is a huge step in healing, although many of us wouldn't label it that way. Just the word "trauma" sounds too severe, too harsh. We might prefer to think of the tragic things that happened to us as "*life.*" Or worse, we may believe we brought it upon our self or somehow deserved it.

There is much research that shows the lifelong effects of trauma include issues with anxiety, panic attacks, depression, and even illnesses like heart disease and diabetes. Most people repeat trauma patterns. For example, a woman who was abused as a child may continue the cycle by entering one abusive relationship after another. The girl who couldn't save her alcoholic father will continue to find herself in relationships with addicts, desperately trying to change the story.

The compounded shock and pain of having two marriages end in infidelity threw me into a significant pit. It was the first time I experienced clinical depression. Regardless, whether we're thrown into the pit or jump into the pit willingly, the darkness and insecurity wreak havoc. I share more about healing through infidelity in the next chapter.

One of the lasting effects childhood trauma had on me was crippling fear and anxiety. I struggled with anxiety all my life without really knowing what it was. I might start sweating like crazy during what felt like a normal conversation with someone, while other times my heart felt like it was going to pound out of my chest. There were other times my head felt strangely hollow, like I was standing outside my body.

Anxiety sucks. One of the best lessons I learned was figuring out simple ways to deal with my anxiety. These are things I (and my kids) use today.

1. *Walk Through It* – Whatever the triggering thought or fear, our minds can get stuck in the "what if's." What if _____ happens again? The thought of "*it*" happening again is overwhelming. So, walk all the way through *it*. If *it* happens again, what will I do? What are the odds of *it* happening again? Would I survive *it* again? What can I do to get help or get out of the situation? Again, walk all the way through *it*. Once you feel empowered, knowing you would survive again, or that the odds are impossible of *it* happening again, you will feel calm. Stronger.

2. *Breathe Through It* – Breathing right is so important. It can rid your brain of the toxic chemicals causing the panic attack or anxiety. Breathe deeply and pay attention to your body. You can also breathe slowly through your nose, counting to seven, then holding your breath for another six or seven seconds. Finally, slowly blow the air out through your mouth for a full eight seconds. Try that multiple times until you feel calm.

3. *Exercise Your Senses Through It* – Tap into your five senses. Point out something you see. A bird in a tree. Then, identify something you hear. Cars driving by. Third, what do you smell? Chlorine from the pool. Next, what are you tasting? The coffee you just finished. Finally, describe something you feel. The hard ground on the back of your legs. Exercising through the senses is called grounding, and it's fabulous.

QUESTIONS TO CONSIDER

Childhood trauma is an important discussion topic. Consider these questions. Take your time; sit with your thoughts, reflect on your history; ask God to guide your memories. Journal your responses.

- Has there been a time you didn't feel safe? Maybe you witnessed a violent event or natural disaster. Was there a time you felt violated or a time you couldn't protect yourself?

- Did you experience a broken home growing up? Were you abused physically, emotionally, or sexually, or possibly neglected as a child?

- Did you lose a parent to death or prison? Did someone struggle with mental illness or addiction in your home?

If you answered yes to any of the questions above, have you given yourself the gift of counseling? If not, it's probably time. And again, *you are worth it.*

CHAPTER TWO

The Desperate Cry for Change

"Though I have fallen, I will rise."
MICAH 7:8

Most of us have experienced trauma of some kind. If not treated, it can present in different ways for years. An affair can, believe it or not, create a kind of trauma. Especially when discovery happens over and over for an extended period. Counselors say one-time disclosure is critical. Details are not necessary and the whole truth should be shared.

Basically, trauma from an affair can be compounded—not only if it happens multiple times—but also when the discovery or disclosure becomes a dripping faucet. The affair partner might feel it necessary to share every ugly detail of their encounter, as often as possible, via email in hopes we'll send him packing and back into her arms. If she's relentless, she may end up at our house or make sure we know the affair is still going strong through social media. Our spouse may begin by telling us there was no physical contact initially, only to admit there was just "that one time" during our next counseling session. Soon we find out they were regulars at a hotel by their office. It is a nightmare. It is devastating, and yes, it is traumatic.

When my counselor first referred to what I was feeling as trauma, the term felt exaggerated. Again, trauma was for soldiers and people who had gone through far worse than what I was experiencing. But, as I had flashbacks of discovery or panicked if my husband had to go to a particular part of town, I began to understand. My anxiety went from zero to sixty in seconds. My thoughts raced, and out of them grew these monstrous, sinister situations. Satan had a field day with my mind for several years, and I had a tough time deciphering what was real and what was just in my head.

I call it "crazy making." Not only do we feel crazy, we act crazy. And, if we're honest, this "crazy" gives our spouse and their affair partner more fuel for the fire. Now they conspire about how insecure and insane we are.

And believe me, you are absolutely justified in your insanity. It's called godly jealousy, and we are entitled to feel it when someone messes with our spouse or children. However, the crazier we feel and become, the less attractive we are, right? At a time when we most want to look "together" and dignified, we come off as an obsessive, crazy, looney-toon. Trust me, I've been there. It's emotionally and mentally draining. Like a bad roller coaster you can't get off, but you must. The sooner the better.

My crazy went on for a long time. And at times, it was *ugly*.

For a while, I quit church. Not God but church. I was isolated. I cried every day, several times a day. The guilt of bringing my children into another disaster felt debilitating. The shame it brought our family and ministry was crippling.

I hadn't touched alcohol in years, but wine helped. The bitter, angry part of me believed I deserved it. Numbing felt better than feeling. As time passed, the collateral damage mounted. Arguing was the way I worked through resentment, and I was overcome with resentment. Our marriage didn't survive. By God's grace, today we're good co-parents and friends. Our son, Luke, I believe is and will be blessed by that.

I can unequivocally say had I not gone through this season, I wouldn't know God like I do. I wouldn't know myself like I do. I wouldn't love myself like I do, and again, that is a gift. There truly is good that can come from suffering. We must seek it and look for it, especially in our questioning.

Breaking the Cycle

I was determined to heal. I knew my old ways of healing weren't going to work this time. I was a pro at "making him sorry." I'm going to assume most of us have gone through a season of making *him* sorry. You know, getting in the best shape you've ever been in and making sure you look all kinds of happy. Today, that's much easier with social media. It reminds me of a quote I reposted recently for girls that says, "Sis, that post isn't going to get his attention. Go write your business plan."

Anyway, I knew how to *show him* what he was missing. I could have focused on revenge and trying to make him sorry. But this time, it wasn't about him. It was about me.

At my lowest point, I honestly didn't think I could live another day in the pain. As I cried one night, questioning the dark thoughts I was having, I begged God to fix me. Not him. Me. This was my pivot point. Overcoming and healing, to the point of changing the negative patterns that helped me survive in the past, took everything I had. The kind of change and healing I'm talking about is not for the faint of heart. *But* it is possible.

The work and self-awareness to drudge through the pain of our past is arduous, grueling work. In fact, you'll want to give up. *Do not.* You must feel the feelings. And I mean, *feel* them. You need to sit in the pain – which is something most of us avoid at all costs.

All the crazy thoughts that keep you in a defeated headspace have to be disproved. Things like, "I'm not pretty enough, sexy enough, thin enough, voluptuous enough." Maybe it's, "I'm not fun enough or wild enough in bed." What's your "not enough?" Please remember, infidelity is not about *you*. People who cheat have their own demons to sort out, and they either will or they won't seek the healing they need. You cannot do it for them, nor can you control or change what they do.

Do whatever it takes to rid these "untruths" from your pretty little head. The voices or messages in your mind that drive you crazy were most likely there before this season. We tend to pick them up in childhood because of something someone said to us or because of the way we felt after being abused or neglected. The message becomes like an old record we replay in our head over and over again. Satan loves to create them and then remind us of them, creating similar storms that trigger the same thoughts. Thoughts that become beliefs, and beliefs that become behavior.

For example: You think, "I'm not enough for him," which leads to you believing, "I'm not lovable." Your behavior then reflects your thoughts and beliefs about who you are. And what do you do? You get back on the abusive, destructive merry-go-round of finding a man who treats you the same way the others did. If you believe you're unlovable, you'll end up in situations or relationships that prove that thought and belief to be true. IT. IS. NOT. TRUE. This cycle needs to be broken and your thinking needs to be recalibrated.

As my marriage was falling apart, I knew in some distant way what God thought and said about me, but I still felt insecure. I constantly heard the mocking voice telling me, "Kim, you're not enough, you'll never be enough." So I sought out and found three ways to heal and fix my screwed-up thinking and doing.

First, I got into serious counseling. I had a counselor who was zealous for my recovery. She was tough, but right, always right. And she pointed me to Jesus.

If you can't tell, I am a huge advocate for counseling. Therapy is important. We all have junk that needs to be processed with a professional that can help us make sense of our patterns and negative behaviors. There is absolutely no shame in seeking help. None. When I expressed my inability to financially afford therapy, my counselor asked me if I would find a way to pay for cancer treatment if I was diagnosed with cancer. "Absolutely," I said. Sometimes, it's that important.

Second, I took a deep dive into scripture to see what Jesus said about me. I also felt it was important to find out what made me happy, apart from a man. After sitting in my pain, I would go find a verse that promised me I was chosen by God. That I was His beloved. I did more of what made me happy, like playing with my kids, listening to music, or going for a long walk. I realized God was continuing to mold me into the woman He created me to be, and part of that meant feeling the pain.

Third, I joined a support group for women. This is one of the best things I did. I had tried Al-Anon and even AA (Alcoholics Anonymous) years before, but they never felt right for me. Not so in this group of women; maybe it was my desperation to get healthy, or perhaps it was finding the right group. Whatever it was, I had a sense of belonging. They were speaking my language from the very first day. With every feeling or experience shared by someone, I wanted to yell, "Me too!"

I began to feel better. To feel hopeful.

I won't lie, the first time walking into a support group of any kind can be unnerving. But when we're determined to break the insanity cycle, we walk through the door. Taking that one uncomfortable step takes courage. It also tells our psyche that our heart matters. And it does.

I loved my women's group. It was safe. The not so ironic thing was, I had been running support groups for teens for years. I had seen the positive impact a group could have. I knew the magic and healing that happened when young people felt accepted and understood. In my women's group I felt understood. It's also the place where I got real – real with myself, real with others, and real with God. I finally took off my "people pleaser" hat and stopped hiding behind the woman I thought the world wanted me to be. My guard came down. It was raw. It was intimate, and it was healing.

In the pit, we can't see a bit of beauty amid the miserable pile of ashes surrounding us. But the beauty is there, and I promise God will bring it forth. Beauty from ashes is one of the greatest things He does.

Sailing with Jesus

There's been nothing normal or smooth about my journey with Jesus, but I've learned there rarely is. It certainly hasn't been like the white-picket-fence I thought it would be. Looking back, I can see how His favor was with me through my "undoing." He brought me through the fire, actually through every storm. His blessings did cover me. Not because I deserve His blessing (and favor), but because He loves me. He loves you.

In my stubbornness, God has proven to be incredibly longsuffering with children as hardheaded as me. I tried everything. In my efforts to be okay, I bounced from one compulsive behavior to the next. Some were good, like running miles on end and working on my relationship with Jesus. Others were not so good, like drinking too much and looking for my identity in men.

The true remedy for my inner pain and turmoil
was, is, and forever will be, Jesus.

So, did I finally heal and make progress? I did. One baby step at a time. It wasn't easy, and it wasn't quick. In fact, I healed not only from this unbelievable, painful train wreck, I also healed from all the ones before it. It still feels miraculous, honestly.

> *Beautiful One,* if you're there or if you have been, my heart hurts for you. I am sorry. There has been no other pain for me like the pain of betrayal. Please don't

go through it alone. And do not believe your cheating spouse can be the friend or support you need to help you process all you are going through. You deserve the help your heart is telling you that you need. You deserve and need to know you are loved immensely and unconditionally, precisely the way you are. God didn't make a mistake. He's incapable of that. You are beautiful and strong and capable. You are worthy and *enough*. Promise me you won't shrink back from that girl I just described, ever. And if you are shrinking back now, please stop. This world needs you to be the woman you were created to be. Whatever it may take to find her again, do it.

LESSONS LEARNED

As I was praying about the lessons I learned during this season, an exercise from my sponsor came to mind. In some respects, this helped me more than the years of counseling, though please remember that counseling is crucial. Every morning, for months, I talked with my sponsor, Pammie. She and I walked through the following questions and answers daily. I'm including answers to each question to give you an idea of what this exercise looks like.

Question: What are two positive emotions you're feeling?
My Answer: Hopeful and grateful.

Question: What are two negative emotions you're feeling?
My Answer: Sad and alone/lonely.

Question: What do you need most today?
My Answer: Comfort and peace.

Question: How can you get that need met without another person or substance?
My Answer: Read Psalms.

Question: What's one tangible thing you can do for *you* today?
My Answer: Workout.

Question: What are two things you're grateful for today?
My Answer: My kids and my patio.

Question: What's your affirmation for today?
My Answer: I will be okay.

I added the gratitude question because gratitude changes our perspective, and I'm a huge fan of finding our blessings. Through this exercise, I found it easier to sit in and process my feelings when I could recognize and name them. I also stopped looking for someone or something to satisfy my needs. *And* I learned to change my *stinkin' thinkin'*. No one can defeat me faster than me. It was during the climb out of the pit that I saw the destruction of negative self-talk and the power in changing it.

If you have untruths stuck in your head, work on them. Don't you dare fall for the lies in your head one more day. Remind yourself of who God says you are. *God says you are Chosen. You are His Daughter. His Beloved. An Heir with Christ. A Conqueror. A Warrior. Forgiven. Redeemed. Delighted in. Free.*

I don't know about you, but I only have to reflect on those truths for a few minutes in order to stand a little taller and smile a little bigger. For years, my favorite thing to say to my girls was, "Remember who you are!" I wanted them to know that no matter who the world told them they were, they were daughters of *the* King. That they mattered.

No one can rob you of the truth once you believe it. And I mean believe it deep in your soul. Believe it to the point that you walk in it. Write your truth on your arm. Tattoo it somewhere if needed. Stick notes on your mirror or in your car. Replace every lie with truth. Daily. Until it sticks.

Live like *you* matter. Even if you're beginning today.

QUESTIONS TO CONSIDER

- Are you at a crossroads? Are you desperate for change? Do you feel like you'll break if things don't change?

- What are the untruths you're believing? Where did they come from? What truth do you need to replace them with?

- Commit to work through the 7 questions from the Lessons Learned for the next few days to reset your *stinkin' thinkin'*?

    1. What are two positive emotions you're feeling? Can you name them? Can you sit in them?
    2. What are two negative emotions you're feeling? Can you name them? Can you sit in them
    3. What do you need most today?
    4. How can you get that need met without another person or substance?
    5. What's one tangible thing you can do for you today?
    6. What are two things you're grateful for today?
    7. What's your affirmation for today?

You've got this girl. You absolutely have it in you. You are worth deep self-examination, and counseling, and safe spaces.

CHAPTER THREE

Back to the Beginning

"You're going to be happy," said life, "but first I will make you strong."
UNKNOWN

For a long time, it was hard to remember the good experiences from my childhood. I seemed to only remember the bad, at least that is - until a whole lot of healing took place. It was a relief to work through childhood trauma because the healing allowed good memories to flood my mind. And there had been a lot of good.

I studied the effects childhood trauma has on the brain when I started working with teens. The topic of trauma was exploding on the addiction front and it was fascinating to learn about how it can rewire pathways in our brains. Many say when trauma happens, we remember bits and pieces of the event with strange clarity. There are very succinct memories amid a heavy fog. That was the case with me.

My mom was a stay-at-home mom and she was devoted to us. Our house was the place to be. I have vivid memories of my mom baking chocolate chip cookies. They're pretty famous with our friends and family. I love music because of my mom. We listened to everything from Motown to Fleetwood Mac to the Eagles. Saturdays, Mom would open the windows, turn up her music, and clean house. (A tradition that is still therapy for me *and* my girls today.)

Another favorite memory was going with my dad to open houses. He was a custom home builder, and I loved his houses. The newness, the architecture, and the piles of dirt and lumber my brother, Eric, and I loved climbing over. We'd eat lunch at a drive-in restaurant called Keller's with our windows down and country music playing on the radio.

I have so many happy memories. Donuts from Dunkin Donuts and Mr. Jim's Pizza on the weekends. Riding in the bed of my granddad's pickup truck. Drinking Shirley Temples at the Country Club. Going for Dairy Queen Dip Cones just because. Catching fireflies at night and playing dig dong ditch with neighbors that knew it was us. And, of course, Dallas Cowboys on Sundays. Football is big in the south, you know.

My Precious Gammie Ruthie

Like most kids, my very best memories are of my Gammie, my maternal grandmother. My parents were hip and young, still enjoying nights and weekends out with their friends, so many weekend nights my brother and I stayed with Gammie. It was the most magical place on earth.

Built in the 1950s, her tiny, white frame house sat at the corner of Avenue G in Garland, Texas, and held more fun than we could stand on the weekends. We loved going to the dime store at the end of the block where we bought bottled Cokes and Bottle Caps, or maybe Fun Dips.

A widow when my mom was just 14, Gammie poured her time and love into Eric and me. If we weren't climbing trees, we were racing Matchbox cars through the dirt or playing croquet outside. Inside, we played checkers or marbles, and sometimes the card game, Go Fish.

We ate handfuls of M&M's poured into a small, white, vintage bowl on Gammie's coffee table. Dinner was usually fried chicken or potpie. As a treat, she might surprise us with Libby's T.V. Dinners. We would finish eating ice cream topped with chocolate syrup while watching Lawrence Welk or Hee Haw. (I was mesmerized by all the bubbles filling the dancefloor of Lawrence Welk and wanted to be the cute, peppy blond with pigtails in that cornfield of Hee Haw.)

My house didn't feel like Gammie's. I was confident we had a ghost in the house. My friends and I played a game called Bloody Mary, messed with the Ouija Board, and watched scary episodes of the Twilight Zone. I'm fairly certain all played a role in the constant fear I felt as a little girl.[2] Nightmares were a pretty regular thing. After a nightmare, I would wake up frozen, unable to move. When I got the courage to breathe, I would count to ten and scream for my dad. God bless him. There's no telling how many nights he laid beside my bed with his hand on my back until I fell back asleep.

Gammie's house was probably the reason I fell in love with the country. She loved having her windows open as much as Mom did. We slept with a big fan making white noise and woke up to a rooster crowing from a farm down the street. Christian talk radio was always on in the kitchen.

My grandmother was the epitome of precious. Ruthie, as the world called her, had the sweetest laugh. She was kind and good. I honestly don't remember anything negative coming out of her mouth. She didn't cuss, she didn't drink, and she never smoked. To me, she was perfect. Her love felt unconditional. She was a true Proverbs 31 woman, and while I didn't know what that was growing up, today I know what a gift her influence was. The imprint she made is undeniable, and I'm certain she'll be the first one to greet me when I get to Heaven.

Gammie's role in my journey is so much more significant than her love for me or the example she set.

Gammie anchored me. She also convinced me God is real.

The Thing Movies Are Made Of

We lived in a nice neighborhood. Eric and I walked to school together every day and roamed the streets for hours. Our house (albeit small) was ideal. Mom went overboard decorating my room, and our home was beautiful because of her natural gift for interior design. However, one fall day, our neighborhood became the thing horror movies are made of.

Friday, October 14, 1977, started out like every other Friday. Well, almost. Our parents were out of town, and Gammie was staying with us. We did walk to school that day like most days. I'm sure we were excited it was Friday and we could buy cupcakes after school. The day was sunny and warm. I remember that.

As we turned the corner at the carpool drop-off, there she was with her big brown eyes and her beautiful, contagious smile. Her smile lit up a room. It was like she beamed from the inside out. The car door opened, and Todd jumped out. He had been too late to walk and was in a hurry. She reminded him of his haircut after school. They lived just a street over from us. Todd's mom, Nancy, held out her arm and motioned for me to give her a hug. Like I said, my parents were out of town for a few days, and she must have known I needed a hug.

Before I go further, let me tell you about Nancy. She was gorgeous, fun, full of energy, and super strong. She and my mom were soul sisters. Inseparable since Todd and I had been born (one week apart), I didn't know life without Nancy and Todd. We were together day and night. They were part of us.

I remember Nancy's laugh, much like I do Gammie's. Nancy loved music and dancing. Determined to help me overcome my fear of June bugs, she frequently put them down my bathing suit. It only took her calling me out one time picking my nose in public to cure that bad habit. She was the cool mom. She was the first person I wanted to show my new haircut because she would go on and on about how cute I was. The day I made cheerleader for the first time, Mom drove me straight to Nancy's house. Of course, she was as excited as I was.

Nancy was athletic. She and Mom played tennis all the time. They took us to the children's theatre, Breakfast with Santa, you name it, and we did it. Life was always fun. It was good. Nancy was also a single mom. Something I admired many years later. She was devoted, like my mom, and very loving and affectionate. I envied Todd because she would let him drive the car around the block (in her lap, of course). She just had a natural way about her that made you happy when you were with her.

Back to that Friday morning. I jumped in Nancy's orange Volkswagen Beetle to hug her. I still remember her hug. While writing this, it occurred to me that she didn't rush me out of the car that day. Many moms would have been worried about the cars behind them. Not Nancy.

That afternoon my dad's mom, Grandma, picked Eric and me up early from school. She said we needed to run out to my granddad's truck stop in Lancaster. We didn't mind because we loved admiring all the big 18-wheelers and seeing Grandpa. Driving back, we passed our neighborhood. Naturally looking down Nancy's street, which came first, I saw cars with lights. We were going too fast for me to see everything clearly, but it looked like multiple police cars were in front of Nancy and Todd's house. As we passed our street, there was a police car in front of our house.

We didn't have cell phones and the drive to Grandma's seemed to take hours. I immediately called our next-door neighbors when we got to Grandma's house. When she answered the phone, our neighbor Margaret sounded upset. Her husband quickly grabbed the phone saying, "Kimmie, someone killed Nancy. She's dead."

Everything went black. I don't remember anything from that moment until Gammie got to Grandma's house. I just remember sitting on the couch, crying.

At ten, I learned the world wasn't safe and that evil was real.

Nancy was brutally murdered. They didn't find her killer, and that made our neighborhood feel unsafe for a long time. Police visited our house multiple times, and there was a lot of "hushing" going on by the adults. At ten, we tend to fabricate our own theory and story based on the bits and pieces we hear.

Eric and I stayed at Gammie's for a few days. Mom was devastated and in no shape to take care of a ten and seven-year-old. Sitting on her curb, I told Gammie I hated God. I hated God for killing Nancy. She didn't scold me. I remember her gently pulling me close and telling me that God didn't kill Nancy. She told me that God loved Nancy, and He loved me. Fear gripped me for years, but somehow, I trusted that truth. I believed Gammie, and I believed God loved me.

Gammie was my anchor. I could do no wrong in her eyes, nor could she in mine. That day, she introduced me to the One who would forever be my Anchor. There would be many lost years before I would finally grasp and understand God's love for me. But that day, a seed was planted by Gammie. A seed to know God that eventually took root. And, despite the loss and fear both my mom and I felt when Nancy was murdered, her influence on my life created a deep desire to chase the good and live life to the fullest.

LESSONS LEARNED

The term self-care is thrown around a lot today. But, do you really know what self-care looks like? It's not as simple as taking a bubble bath or going to the spa, while both are splendid and important. Self-care is actually planning and committing to taking care of your needs every day, not just on a special occasion or after a major meltdown. Trust me, I know a great number of you have become experts at taking care of others, putting your needs last. I get it. I did it for years.

In processing my childhood stuff, I learned the importance of healing and acknowledging my inner child. Sound odd? She's there, and she needs you to see and hear her. Whether you experienced the death or abandonment of a parent, physical, sexual, or emotional abuse, maybe a long-term illness of some kind – the little girl in you needs you to validate what she went through. What she felt.

Are you a "fixer" – or always people pleasing, seeking external validation from others? Do you stay on high alert, afraid something horrible is about to happen? Do you tolerate abuse you know you shouldn't?

Many of us, for many different reasons, were forced to grow up too early. Something robbed our innocence or caused us to feel like we were responsible for someone else's wellbeing. In doing so, we missed opportunities to just be kids or to heal.

What did you love to do when you were little? Did you love to create? Go buy a coloring book and color. Pick up a canvas and paint. Don't worry about the finished product (especially my perfectionist friends). Get lost in the activity.

Did you love music growing up? Go for a drive with the windows down and music turned up loud. Sing at the top of your lungs. Go to the park and blow bubbles or swing on the swing set. Ride a bike. Fly a kite. Go get an ice cream or hot fudge Sunday for heaven's sake. You get my point. I'm 100 percent serious. Go do things that make the little girl in you happy.

Finally, commit to take care of your needs every single day. Set those boundaries. Slow down your "yes," as Rachel Hollis says. She also hosted an amazing challenge one summer, inspiring me to drink half my body weight in water, to move my body every single day, and get good sleep. And guess what? I still do it every day. Get out in the sunshine. Take up a new hobby. Feed your soul. Laugh!

Because why?

That's right! *You're worth it.*

QUESTIONS TO CONSIDER

Looking at our childhood and the things or events that shaped us is important. Both the good and the bad. It's also crucial to our healing, the quality of our lives, and our relationships.

- Spend a day reflecting on your childhood, remembering who you were, who you wanted to be. Think about the things you loved. What made you happy?

- What needs weren't met for you as a child? Who taught you what a woman looks like? What about a man? Are there behaviors or emotions you get stuck in today that result from those unmet needs or beliefs?

- Are there places in your little girl heart that need attention? Are there people who were positive role models you should thank? What are three things you can begin doing to take better care of yourself? What do you most want to incorporate into your daily self-care routine?

Do it!

CHAPTER FOUR

The Lost Years

"Oh, my darling, it's true. Beautiful things have dents and scratches too."
UNKNOWN

Sexual abuse almost always creates a message of worthlessness. In adolescence, we may end up with boys that use us, affirming that "worthless" message. As young women, sex begins to equal love in our mind, only it doesn't, and the message just gets louder. As adults, we may doubt men and their intentions, even the best of men. Somehow, men and women alike seem to all accept the message we're hell-bent to live out. Remember, what we think we believe and what we believe (about ourselves) becomes our destiny.

I believe Satan sets out to defeat and destroy us from an early age. His tactic being to create the untruths we take on and believe and operate from. If there's one thing I know, it's that Satan is predictable. He will find ways to repeat that message that cripples you as often as he can. It may come in a new and different package, but the result and message are the same. Defeat. One of my favorite pastors, Pastor Rod, described it to me this way:

When you were born, God beamed down with pride, full of love for you. His creation. His child. Just as He did, Satan stood not far off, also taking note of your beauty. He said to his emissaries, "She may be a tough one. We need to start early. If sexual abuse doesn't destroy her, work on her parents, divorce will disillusion her. If divorce doesn't work, try abuse and addiction. Make sure she's introduced to drugs at her lowest point, and then be sure she's used over and over by men. If that doesn't work, lure her husband into an affair and in the process take out her kids. That should do it."

Satan knows your potential. He knows what you can become, and he fears that. He is cunning and a master at sending destruction wrapped up in a beautiful package, looking like everything you've always wanted. For me, most of his attempts came through men and my need to be loved. Far too early, I bought the lie that sex equals love, only it doesn't.

When we're exposed to sexual behavior before we're developmentally ready, it can become tied to feelings of comfort or love. This intertwining of feelings and behavior are too difficult for a child to sort through. Shame is a given. So is the loss of innocence. At a young age, we learn our body isn't our own and physical boundaries don't exist.

As hard as I've tried, I cannot remember the first time sexual behavior entered my life. I know it had to be early because I don't remember life before it. Children engaging in behavior far worse than the typical, "Show me yours, and I'll show you mine." I believe it can happen when a child is being abused by an adult and then recreates the same behavior with siblings, cousins, or friends. My parents never knew and my secrecy fueled the shame. The shame fueled my untruths. It was the beginning of a dark hole inside that begged for years to remain numb.

As a little girl, I was praised for being pretty and sweet. I was very affectionate. I didn't consider anyone a stranger and loved hugging everyone. I still do. Good or bad, and despite the dark moments, I never felt like anything was missing from my life. I had terrific parents. There wasn't a single day I didn't hear, "I love you." Whatever our world, it was my norm.

In middle school, my parents divorced and I was heartbroken about my dad moving out. Obviously, divorce is hard on kids, but I cannot imagine my family being any different than it is today. We have been blessed as a blended family. My Daddy Keith is one of the most precious gifts God has ever given me. He not only helped raise me, he stepped in and helped raise my daughters, Haleigh and Anna. To this day, I believe he is the one man on this planet who has never let them down.

My dad remarried a strong, bold British woman, Annie, who brought fire and excitement into our lives. I gained sisters I can't imagine doing life without. They helped me accept truths I didn't want to see, laugh until I nearly peed my pants, cried with me over stupid boys, and served as my partner in crime during my "lost years." Again, I wouldn't trade a thing.

The Lost Years

I have scattered memories impacted by trauma. While my childhood had a lot of happy memories mixed in with a few painful ones, high school and college didn't have as many happy moments. Thus, I call these "the lost years."

My love for approval (or applause) fit well with cheerleading. I loved cheerleading. I apologize now for any of you who had bad experiences with cheerleaders. Clearly, people tend to either hate us or love us.

Approval also meant being part of the student council, making A/B honor roll, and receiving other honors throughout high school. I was, as they say, attracted to "bad boys" - like a moth to a flame actually. Whatever that draw, I was a magnet. Most were partiers, and I didn't discriminate between addictions. As long as drama and "saving" were part of the equation, I was in.

I didn't understand fully what it meant to be addicted to addicts, a "co-addict" so it's called, until I started the recovery process during my S.H.A.T.T.E.R.I.N.G. season. While my *bad boy* was fixated on the next high, be it cocaine or sex, I was fixated on him and every move he made. In complete honesty, most of the boys I dated were just as broken as me. Remember, baggage begets baggage. Subconsciously we hoped the other person might heal parts of us that were hurting or broken.

We were living out the lies about ourselves,
those untruths we had come to believe as children.

Each relationship shaped me in one way or another. I'm a huge believer that good can always come from bad. Failed relationships have the potential to teach us about ourselves, especially what we want and don't want in a partner. I'm sure that works both ways. We'd be wise to accept we simply can't be *it* for every man on this planet. That it's actually okay to not be chosen. Sometimes even a good thing. Unanswered prayers, right?

For years, I thought I would marry my high school sweetheart. Eight years off and on, our romance included poems, love letters, and an endless list of songs. He was a senior. I was a freshman. And yes, *my mama tried.* Getting caught up in the Romeo and Juliet saga just makes you believe your fairytale is bound to come true, doesn't it? I sure did. Although we broke up my senior year of high school, we got back together in college when he called and needed "saving." We got engaged soon after. As would become a repeating pattern, he found another gal and I was devastated.

Betrayal #1

Romance and relationships felt like one train wreck after another, honestly. Some involved emotional and physical abuse, most involved too much partying, one a pregnancy, and of course, my ever-growing pit deep within kept expanding. Demanding to be filled. So, fill it I did. Boys, alcohol, food, and even working out did the trick for a little while, but nothing worked for long. My untruths played out with every choice I made.

The amazing thing is, I see God's hand on me the entire time. Sound crazy? Let me explain.

I have sweet memories of my mom reading Bible stories to me as a little girl. She told me recently that she and Nancy taught our Sunday school class right before Nancy's death. I remember Vacation Bible School at First Baptist Church in Garland and going to fellowship hall with Gammie at First Methodist Church.

Our family stopped going to church when I was in 5th grade. It took me years to understand my mom's personal struggle with God during that time. She lost her dad at 14. For a daddy's girl that adored her father, she was devastated. Living through Nancy's murder was nothing short of horrific. While she never lost her faith, she had her reasons to be angry with God. I fully understand that now.

Funny how life works that way, isn't it? I love my parents more every year. Their ways and rules, and even their reactions to my childhood and teenage behaviors, all seemed to make much more sense as my daughters grew up. I can't tell you how many times my girls tried to leave the house wearing just about nothing only to think, "Ahhhh, that's why Mom looked at me that way."

In middle school, I went to church camp with my best friend, Dana. We both experienced the proverbial mountain top and came home saved. For those who haven't heard that term, it means giving your heart and life to Jesus and committing to follow Him.

For whatever reason, I didn't tell my family about being saved at camp or about the baptism ceremony planned that Sunday upon returning from camp. I can't explain why I decided not to acknowledge it or get baptized. I just didn't. In my internal psyche, I felt like my hesitancy to be baptized disappointed God. I failed His test, so to speak, in my young mind. The untruths settled in even deeper. Now, I wasn't measuring up in God's eyes. I didn't have the Biblical words or even understanding to call it denying God, but I felt like I let Him down.

For a long time, I resigned myself to the idea that God cared much more about church people than us non-churched people. When we're not exposed to the Bible, and so many of us weren't as kids, we make up all kinds of things about God. Most of my friends didn't go to church or talk about the Bible, so it was easy to revert to the way things were. And we did revert back, but something in me had changed. I was still an approval addict with all kinds of mistakes ahead of me, but there was a tug on my heart toward God.

In high school, I gravitated to Young Life. My boyfriend and I visited a church just outside of town with his family and ended up getting baptized there. I loved the way I felt in church or when I sensed God's presence. I didn't know Him, but I knew He was real. I knew He loved me, and that made me love Him in some unexplainable way. The seed Gammie planted was taking root.

Worthless. Invisible. Unlovable.

My senior year in high school, I decided I needed to "play the field." I ended up in an abusive relationship that brought excruciating trauma into my life. By the time I got to college, I was broken and did what most broken college girls do. I drank. A lot. Drugs soon followed. So did more bad boys and a season of self-loathing– a spiraling. It took years of therapy to find even one positive memory from college. My choices nearly destroyed me.

At Texas Tech, I was awarded Best Pledge for my sorority. While my attempts at sorority life failed miserably, God blessed me with a Big Sister named Brenda, who just happened to be the godliest girl on campus, or at least that's how I saw her. She was President of the sorority and ended up appointing me Chaplin. Yes, I see the humor, but I also see God's outrageous love. While I had been exposed to God and church, I certainly knew nothing about the Bible, nor had I ever prayed out loud. I'm actually pretty sure I didn't even know what a "Chaplin" was when Brenda appointed me.

Gammie had given me a Bible when I left for college. I think it had been a gift to my parents when they got married. During my first semester of college, a friend suggested I read Psalms and Proverbs. They were easier to read and made more sense than some of the other books in the Bible. Somehow, in my insecurity, I mustered the courage to share scripture and pray on Monday nights with my sorority sisters. You could say it was my first stint at public speaking, and it was no coincidence I was sharing Jesus.

In hindsight, God was there, weaving a beautiful tapestry into even the most shame-inducing season of my life.

The conflict within isn't hard to see, is it? I wanted to do the right thing, desperately. I just kept spiraling. It was like the black hole created by shame demanded to be fed, and I felt obliged to feed it.

My choices and partying led to being in the wrong place at the wrong time one night, and my spiraling ended by being raped by two guys I thought were my friends. I still have a difficult time putting into words what this was like. Again, I didn't tell my parents. I did tell them I was scared of the path my life was taking with drugs. My self-loathing hit a bottom, and as soon as I made a cry for help, my dad put my brother on a plane so he could drive me to California. I lived with my dad and stepmom, Annie, for a little while. It was good to clear my head and be away.

Betrayal #2

After months of sitting out of college, I knew I wanted to go back to Texas Tech and finish my last semester. I did, and as soon as I got there I ran into a big, burly football player I had met a year earlier. We had a blast together at Tech. After graduation, most of our friends were taking the next step and planning weddings. Marriage whispered the hope of growing up and leaving a painful past behind. So, we did it. He was my first husband. Mom created the most perfect, princess-like wedding you could imagine. Gammie was sick and in the hospital the night we got married. One of my favorite memories is having the limo driver run by the hospital before we headed to the reception. The looks we got were priceless, but nothing compared to the way Gammie beamed and sat straight up in bed when she saw us.

After our wedding, we moved to Lubbock, Texas to work for friends. Both daughters were born in west Texas. Haleigh, my firstborn, changed me – or saved me, however you want to look at it. She had a small bit of sass but was completely angelic. Our second daughter, Anna, was pure sunshine. Joy. She never stopped smiling and she saved me in a different way.

A few days after delivering our second daughter, I was faced with the reality that my husband was having an affair. An affair he wasn't sure he wanted to leave – thus, betrayal #2.

So, with a two-year-old and a seven-week-old in tow, I loaded up the biggest U-Haul they had and headed back to Dallas. Mom says that was the moment she knew I could handle anything life threw at me. I still wasn't so sure, but the overcomer kicked in, and we were off. I relate that drive to, "Jesus Take the Wheel" by Carrie Underwood.

Things were definitely in a bit of a fog for a while. I moved in with Mom and Daddy Keith. I remember Anna's constant smile and Haleigh's playfulness. Scared to death, I still knew somehow, we were going to be okay. God would take care of us, and He did.

Growing up with a single mom is not easy for kids. It wasn't for mine, howbeit they were exceptional children. I'm sure I'm biased, but we had fun and made the best of our life. It was us against the world. There was something resilient in the three of us, and I think we all believed it was because we had each other. Today, our bond is one of the most beautiful things in my life, and without question, unbreakable.

> *Sister,* I've lived long enough to know we all have days we'd rather forget. Days when evil overshadowed anything good. Days, or nights, we wish we didn't have stuck in our minds. Times we hoped God wasn't watching. If you have that movie reel playing over and over in your head, reminding you of your mistakes, it's time to work through your past. My prayer is that you overcome every bit of shame you've carried. I pray you will not only see but experience that good can come from evil. Sometimes we need help finding it. Healing comes from looking at our past, even the days we spent in the pit. It's important to understand how we got there and why we thought so little of ourselves. Finding the answer to this *why* is essential. So is looking for God's hand on your life. Trust me, it has been there all along.

LESSONS LEARNED

Well, it's hard to reflect on this chapter and not be like, "*Duh*, my greatest lesson learned *ever* was the importance of Salvation." I'm not sure I would have survived the lost years if I hadn't been introduced to Jesus. While I wish I would have learned about Him by studying the Bible earlier in my life, I know His hand on me saved me, repeatedly.

Have you taken that step and given your heart to Jesus? If you haven't, and your heart is pounding or maybe you feel a little anxious, it might be God drawing you into a relationship with Him. Before we go any further, I want to share very simply how you can do just that.

Some folks (or churches) believe you have to say a certain prayer, while others don't. Some believe you have to be baptized and others don't. Some baptize by sprinkling, others by dunking. Again, I have to state that I am not a theologian nor a Bible teacher. What I know is the Bible says in Romans 10:9, "For if you publicly declare with your mouth that Jesus is Lord and believe in your heart that God raised him from the dead, you will experience salvation."

If you want to invite Jesus into your life and heart, here are three simple steps to pray through. Take your time – there's no magic words or formula. This is truly a moment in time where your heart and spirit are connecting with the heart and spirit of God. Breathe.

1. Admit you have sin in your life. (We all do! We always will.) Ask God to forgive you of your sins.

2. Search your heart. Do you believe that Jesus is the Son of God? Do you believe He died on the Cross, as the perfect and

ultimate sacrifice so you can go to Heaven? Do you believe Jesus was raised from the dead on the third day, proving that He is Lord? If so, simply tell God you believe in Jesus and the price He paid for you on the Cross. Thank Him.

3. Ask Jesus to come live in your heart and life.

Wow! If you just invited Jesus into your life and heart, congratulations! I believe it is the best decision you will ever make. Maybe you've already prayed a prayer. Maybe it's just time to invite God to be the Lord of your life again. Whatever it is at this point in your journey, know I've prayed for you. I trust God is going to move in your life in mighty ways.

I can't wrap up this Lessons Learned without telling you to start reading the Bible and find a group of godly women to get plugged in with. I've grown the most studying and reading the Bible. And, I'll be honest, reading it was hard for me. It didn't make a lot of sense. For what it's worth, it's good to start in Matthew and read through the New Testament. If you start in the first chapter of Genesis and try to read straight through the Bible, you might not stick with it. And then you might! Pray your way through. God will guide you.

I love the devotional, Jesus Calling. Here is a website for that daily devotional: Jesuscalling.com. I also highly recommend Beth Moore Bible studies. Her writing changed my life. *And*, side note, I was beyond blessed to cross meeting her off my bucket list last year. She's even more precious in real life, and it was amazing to thank her face to face.

QUESTIONS TO CONSIDER

We all have years we struggled through, maybe even years or seasons we regret. We're human and flawed and need Jesus. At least that's what I'm going to keep telling you.

- Do you have days or seasons you've tried to bury? Have you accepted those days or seasons as events or people that taught you about life? About who you are or want to be?

- Has God been chasing you? Can you see His hand on your life and the ways He showed up even in the times you felt distant from Him?

- Where does your hope come from? Your inner peace?

We all need hope. We all seek peace. Explore it. Take time to think through your answers and what your heart is most longing for right now.

CHAPTER FIVE

White Picket Fences

"We are all broken, that's how the light gets in."

ERNEST HEMINGWAY

The one thing I knew or hoped would make a difference in the girls' lives – being raised by a single mom – was church. Remember, in my belief, church meant God's favor. Church was the answer. Therefore, we joined a church, and I moved from the lost years to the church years.

One of my childhood friends who seemly came from one of those perfect, white-picket-fence homes, suggested we try the church he and his family attended. It was a nearby Methodist church. The girls and I tried it and joined immediately. I went through the Divorce Care class, was counseled by one of the pastors, and started volunteering in the three-year old Sunday school class. While Anna was happy-go-lucky everywhere we went, Haleigh felt safer if I was within eyeshot.

If you haven't picked up on it, I love to lead. Gammie always told me I was bossy, as if it was a good thing. Within no time, I was leading a single parent's class at church. Again, can you see the humor? I still didn't know anything really about the Bible. Yet, God in His goodness (and humor) allowed me to lead. In all honesty, part of me hoped I might meet a godly man in class.

In time, life got in the way, and I stopped teaching. Climbing the corporate ladder and raising two active girls kept me running. After about a year's absence from church, my neighbor, Scott, suggested I try his church, Bent Tree Bible Fellowship in Carrollton, Texas. I was in a weird space mentally and Scott knew it. I was happy with my life. I loved being a mom. I was successful professionally, and I was in the best physical shape I had ever been in. Yet, still, there was something missing.

Actually, there was a *lot* missing. Truth and integrity to name two. To go a little deeper into my psyche at that time, I had a crush on a married man who had convinced me he was "separated" while living at home. I know, I know. *Stupid.* The truth came out quickly. Thank God!

We all get tripped up by lies at one time or another. Yes, that man may be miserable in his marriage or maybe he's even fallen out of love. But *you* deserve more than being an affair partner. Much more. His wife and kids also deserve more.

Aside from my hideous choices, I was the girl that couldn't wait to buy the December issue of Cosmo. You know, the one with the full year's horoscope. How better to know what I had waiting for me in the year ahead? Bless. I also kept a Magic 8 ball[2] on my desk, often inquiring whether a guy was right for me. Would he call back? Should I like him? I was a hot mess. Thankfully, our Forger can shape even the hottest mess, as long as we're a moldable mess.

The first time I visited Bent Tree, Pastor Pete asked anyone struggling or needing prayer to stand up. Odd, I thought. Every fiber in me said, "Do not stand!" But before I knew it, I was standing, and strangers were moving in to put their hands on me. I stood there, feeling awkward. Though my legs were shaking, I felt so loved by these people, again, complete strangers. A few women even hugged me afterward and said they would continue to pray for me. I knew that day Bent Tree would become the place we called home.

I signed up to serve in a ministry called Promise Land, knowing my attendance average would be much better if I was committed to be there every Sunday. The girls and I served as a traveling mini-worship group, you could say, singing to the little ones. We brought bells and tiny Bibles with us to each class, singing songs like B-I-B-L-E, as well as Jesus Loves Me and I've Got the Joy, Joy, Joy, Joy, Down in My Heart. (It's okay if you want to sing for a minute.) We taught the 18-month to 24-month-olds how to treat and take care of their Bible and why they were so special. I'm pretty sure we all three got more from our trips to each room than the children did. The babies loved singing, and we loved watching them sing.

Bent Tree is where I finally learned about the Bible. I could sit under Pete's teaching for days. I was a complete sponge and wanted to know everything there was to know about God. I fell madly in love with Jesus at Bent Tree. The girls were thriving and happy. I have the sweetest memories of reading Bible stories or memorizing scripture together. My favorite memory is them raising their precious, little hands when we worshipped. As soon as my hands went up, theirs would go up. Life felt good. It finally felt right. God was preparing us.

The Tsunami

We had been at Bent Tree for about a year when life came crashing in. Another tsunami. One that would forever alter Haleigh and Anna's lives.

Their dad had moved to Dallas and things had gone well. He was a big teddy bear, and to them, he was larger than life, fun and affectionate. He was getting married and our daughters couldn't wait to be in the wedding. But this particular summer, something felt "off." He was distant and seemed to be gone a lot. The girls talked about Daddy working nights and sleeping all day. I knew something was wrong and asked God to intervene. He did, within days of my prayer.

At first, I told the girls Daddy was sick. Unfortunately, the truth was he met a girl who introduced him to crystal meth. In an instant, he was hooked, and life changed forever. For him and for us. Then, I told them Daddy was making bad choices and couldn't see them for a while. Nothing made sense to them. All they knew was the Daddy they adored vanished. No goodbye. No reason, and no plan to return.

They searched the crowd at every soccer or tee-ball game they played, every choir concert, and every dance recital. Haleigh became a perfectionist and was hard on herself. Anna would ask, "If I cheer good today, will Daddy come back?" It was devastating. What do you do with that? I could love them, but love didn't fill the void, nor did it answer their questions, especially the untruths being born in their little hearts.

- "Did I do something to make Daddy leave?"
- "What can I do to make him come back?"
- "Am I not lovable?"

Children are egocentric. And no, that doesn't mean prideful. It means they relate things and events to themselves. It is why kids believe they caused their parents' divorce or think they can do something to stop Dad's drinking. In their minds and hearts, they believe they can affect life around them. We prayed for their dad every night. I sincerely don't believe they missed a night.

The Betty Ford Children's Program

They attended the Betty Ford Children's Program, where they learned the Seven C's. I didn't *cause* it. I can't *control* it. I can't *cure* it. But I can take *care* of myself. I can *communicate* my feelings. I can make healthy *choices*. And I can *celebrate* myself.[3]

They had the best counselors and learned "healthy" ways to express their feelings, through things like art or writing. I let them go in their rooms to scream really loud when they were frustrated or angry. They love telling the story of Haleigh duct taping a pillow to Anna to then use as a punching bag. While I did allow punching pillows, this was not part of said therapy. Sisters will be sisters.

We did a lot of things to help them be kids. Children living through trauma often grow up too quickly and miss opportunities to simply be kids. Bike riding, going to the park, getting ice cream, and even blowing bubbles can help.

The girls processed as much as they could at their young ages. I was told they would process at every milestone. At 13, they processed what they could as a 13-year-old. The same happened at 16, 18 and 21. They will continue to process until the little girl inside them is fully healed.

The day their Dad transferred from county jail to state prison was the day my dream for their white picket fences imploded. I sat on their bathroom floor and cried for what felt like hours. I was terrified for them and scared for him.

My Mom and Daddy Keith lived down the street and made sure the girls didn't miss a beat. They were with us all the time, for everything. I overcompensated, which didn't serve any of us well. I volunteered at their school by serving on the PTA board and as room mom. I was cheer coach, dance mom, you name it. We attended every Mother-Daughter event at church, and other churches. They went to camps. We went to worship concerts and on mission trips.

I did everything I could to "fix" it, but nothing could fix the Daddy-Daughter dances they couldn't attend or the pain that came with birthdays and holidays. It was like a death, but it wasn't. Eventually, their dad came back into their lives, and while our parenting styles proved to breed a serious level of contention, they found healing. And at the end of the day, nothing could be better than that.

During this season, the church was our safe place. The small group of teen girls I led became a tiny army of support. The small group leaders of my daughters groups went above and beyond to show them love every week.

Despite the turmoil, God kept His hand on us. The sunflower on the cover of this book is a reminder of that. One morning I had taken the girls to school, and I was utterly overcome with fear. I was reading everything I could about addiction, probably too much. On this particular morning, my fears were hammering me. After I dropped the girls off at school, I drove past a field I had passed a hundred times. For some reason, I paused to look at it. It was like time stood still. The ground in front of me was covered with big, beautiful, yellow sunflowers. It looked like thousands of them. They were huge and seemed to go on for miles. At the back of the field, I could see a Cross.

In a quiet whisper, I heard God speak into my heart, "I love them more than you do, Kim."

Tears flowed. I knew at that moment God had them in *His* grip. I didn't have to worry about their future. (Although I did, many times.) God loved them and had a plan for them. My job was to release them and trust Him.

I've watched my strong, resilient, intelligent, fun, beautiful daughters' process and heal year after year. Today, they amaze me and are my best friends. Two of the greatest things I have ever done. My greatest gifts. Whatever God has for them, I know it will be much better than white picket fences.

> *Moms*, hear me. Our children have to figure things out on their own. They have to fail. They have to experience heartache. They will most likely spend time in the wilderness. We all do. Raise them as if they're going to go through the same heartbreaks you did. Prepare them for the storms. Maybe her perfectionism will lead to the same eating disorder. His depression may lead to the same suicidal thoughts. She may end up pregnant her senior year. Again, prepare them for the storm. And *Precious Mom*, know they see you. They see your work ethic. They see you overcome. They see the way you treat people. The way you take care of yourself. The faith you lean into when times are hard. It is absolutely in our storms that our roots grow deep, and we want their roots to grow deep. Give them to God.

LESSONS LEARNED

Two things occurred to me writing this chapter. Both important. One of the funniest, yet not so funny, things I learned during the church years had to do with boundaries.

When the girls were little, I tried to cram every self-help tactic into their little minds and lives that I could. In hopes of preventing them from having any baggage. Yes, I know that's impossible. It's humorous just thinking about my efforts.

Anyway, boundaries.

I grabbed the book "Boundaries with Kids"[4] as soon as it hit the shelves. Not knowing what the heck boundaries really meant, it was important for my girls to have them. As soon as I started reading the book, I woefully had to admit I didn't have any boundaries. Not a one from what I was reading. Whew! Back to the bookstore I ran to pick up the adult version of Boundaries.[5]

What a concept! I loved the fact that good boundaries meant *not* saying "yes" to everything and everyone. I was the "yes" girl. A new committee, sure. Join our board, absolutely. Take on another project at work, of course. Yes, yes, yes. Until I crashed and burned.

I was horrified to learn I didn't need to tell a man every appalling detail of my past on our first date. Nor did the lady at Macy's need to hear my life story or what I had going on relationally. I learned that people should earn the right to know my stuff. I learned that boundaries are like gates. They keep bad things or people out while allowing the good things and people in.

You always have a choice. If something – or someone – isn't good for your mental health and well-being, you have every right to set a boundary. Maybe you only stay for an hour at Christmas dinner instead of all day because your toxic aunt berates you endlessly. You can say no to helping with the school book fair, and *still* be a good mom. You can miss a night out with friends to stay home and enjoy a bubble bath with a glass of wine.

The best way I know to respect my "yes" problem is to say "no." I heard a speaker say years ago that *unless* our hearts jump out of our chests when someone asks us to join a committee or help with something, we should say, "no." Saying "no!" feels good, and when it feels good, you know it was the right answer. If you get excited about what you're being asked to do or join, then by all means do it.

Healthy boundaries make us, and our kids, better humans.

The second thing I learned during this season was the importance of healthy girlfriends. During my single mom days, I couldn't have survived without my girlfriends. A "tribe" wasn't a thing back then, but Kari, Tiffany, Amy, Karem, and both Jamie's – they were my tribe. You need good girlfriends. Friends you can laugh and cry with. Travel with. Friends who will come over at 3 a.m. when your baby has a 101° fever. Friends who will tell you the guy you just met seems like a creep. Friends who will pray over you before you have that mass removed from you breast. Friends who will celebrate you and sit with you in suffering. Over the years, God added Jessica, two Julie's, Kristen, Ingrid, and Sandy to my tribe. I thank God for my girlfriends and cannot imagine life without them.

QUESTIONS TO CONSIDER

- So much to unpack here. Are you the "yes" girl? Are you exhausted most of the time? Do you cringe when they ask you to take on another project or event, yet still say "yes?" You may want to grab the book *Boundaries* by Dr. Henry Cloud & Dr. John Townsend.

- Who's in your tribe? Who has earned the right to be inside your inner circle? Think about the five people you spend the most time with. Are they people you most want to be like?

If you don't have a tribe or good, trustworthy girlfriends, pray for them. God wants you to have that support and friendship in your life as much as you do. It's just super important that you find people who not only want the best for you, but hold your feet to the fire when you start to get off track.

CHAPTER SIX

The Invisible Children

"Anyone can find the dirt in someone. Be the one who finds the gold."
PROVERBS 11:27

In 2005, Haleigh, Anna and I traveled with two wonderful teenage girls from our church youth group to Uganda, Africa. Both girls were mentoring my daughters at home, and when they asked me if I would consider taking them to Africa, I knew we were supposed to go. A wonderful couple from our church who were missionaries in Kampala, the Capital of Uganda, invited us to stay and work with them. I can't even begin to tell you how much we underestimated all God would teach us during the trip.

Before the trip, our missionary friend Margaret did an excellent job preparing us for the time we'd spend in her village. She urged us to pray that our eyes would be opened to see people and things through God's eyes. I didn't understand what it meant to "see through God's eyes." While it sounded Christian-like, did I really want to see what God saw? My heart wasn't sure, but I prayed for it anyway. We all did.

We were actually in London headed to Africa when the 2005 bombings happened. It's not unusual to spend a day or night layover in London on the trip. It was early morning, and we were determined to ride the subway to see the city for a few hours before catching our flight to Uganda. As we approached the ticket counter, the agent suggested we wait for an hour before catching the subway until after the rush hour passed. During that one hour wait is when the 2005 subway bombings happened. We wondered for days if the ticket agent had been a guardian angel.

While it certainly shook up our families at home, we were convinced God was watching over our trip.

Honestly, I felt at home the minute we landed in Uganda. I can't explain it. It was mid-day and hot, and it looked the way I imagined a third world country would look. While the poverty struck me, I wasn't surprised by anything we saw. Well, except for the tiny, naked children wandering around alone. They couldn't be more than three or four years old. There were older children, at most eight or ten year's old, carrying babies around. They seemed happy, oblivious to the poverty. Kids were laughing and playing in the streets. It was loud and a bit chaotic, especially driving through the city. Horns were honking and people were yelling at each other. I knew we had to totally trust God to survive the traffic circles. Yet, in the madness of Uganda, I felt at home. I loved this place and had no idea why.

Our first few days, we worked at different orphanages. We painted a church and gave our testimonies. The children were mesmerized by Anna. I don't think any of them had seen another child their age with white skin and blonde hair. Haleigh, being in middle school, made fast friends and they wrote and exchanged notes with each other the entire time we were there. The kids in Kampala were full of joy. They laughed and danced. They loved being held and, at any one time, we could count on holding multiple kids in our laps. We blew bubbles and made sock puppets, only for the kids to take the socks and put them on their feet. A luxury we didn't consider when we planned the craft.

We each had different experiences. My moment came the day we went to an orphanage for babies. Truth be told, I always wanted to adopt a black baby. Literally, people in high school would give me pictures of precious black babies because I loved them so much. My parents were shocked that I didn't adopt while we were there. (I seriously contemplated it.)

We spent most of the day at the orphanage - all four girls embraced the opportunity to hold and love on the babies. I was immediately struck by the lack of nurturing. Babies were picked up by one arm and placed on the ground. Alone. It seemed cold to me.

The setting was much like what we had seen in other parts of Uganda. We saw decaying and rundown buildings surrounded by red dirt. An old fence made of rusted iron encircled an area of broken toys and battered swing sets. A clothesline ran across the length of the yard holding laundered, tattered clothes. It was a hot day, and most of the babies wore little clothing. The orphanage workers used and reused cloth diapers. Bottles and cups were old and dirty.

The filth and unsanitary conditions weighed heavy on my heart. Some of the children toddled around, pushing sun-faded toys through the dirt. Babies who hadn't yet learned to walk sat alone in the dirt and dust. Some were crying in cribs or playpens. Few were held.

While touring the office, I noticed a wall covered in chalk writings. At a closer look, each baby was listed on the wall along with the date they came into the orphanage, the best guess of their age, and their physical condition when they arrived. A few had adoption dates at the end of the row. The thought occurred to me that there had to be thousands of children, given the sheer number of orphans in Africa, who may not know their birthday. I couldn't imagine having or being a child who didn't know their own birthday.

Earlier, I spotted Betty, an amazing woman who worked at the orphanage, holding a baby named Mercy Grace. Betty was different from the other workers. She had a lightness about her. She was nurturing and loving on the babies. As I walked up, Betty let me hold Mercy Grace who had gorgeous, big brown eyes and a breathtaking smile. Mercy Grace and I walked the yard for what felt like hours. I couldn't put her down. With every beautiful smile, it seemed she knew I was falling in love with her.

What was her story? I learned that Mercy Grace had been found in a dumpster when she was just a few days old, covered with bugs. I believe they said maggots. I asked about adoption. The process required we stay in Uganda for five to six months, which was something I knew we couldn't do. But all was not lost. As Betty and I talked, she mentioned her own desire to adopt Mercy Grace. She eventually did and has raised Mercy Grace as her own. In fact, her heart is so big she started a nonprofit to help special needs children in Uganda. Did I mention she is an amazing woman?

After our time at the baby orphanage, we piled into our dusty, hot van, and drove back to the house for dinner. I replayed image after image of the children in their cold, dirty environment with no mommy or daddy to hold them when they cried, to love them, or rock them to sleep. It seemed unconscionable. How could this happen in any place on our planet? I thought about caring for my own daughters and how every need was met. I had held them for hours to make sure they felt safe and loved.

My heart broke. I cried uncontrollably for a long time. Weeping. I had seen through God's eyes. That day, I felt the Holy Spirit grieve over the condition and care of those babies. We had prayed God would break our hearts for what breaks His, and He did.

Invisible Children

In 2006 we returned to Uganda. This time, it was me, the girls, seven teens from our youth group, and a male leader named Mark. That year we learned about Joseph Kony and the terror he was causing around a city called Gulu. We watched the Invisible Children Documentary and knew we wanted to go work in the area. Our drive from the airport to Gulu would take a good part of the day. We were all a little uncomfortable when we learned men with guns would be escorting us. And yes, it looked just like you see on T.V. or in movies. One of our vans broke down in route, and the reality of just how dangerous the area we were driving through sunk in.

We could feel a heaviness in the air as soon as we got to Gulu. The gravity of evil could be heard during the night as I prayed, lying awake and hoping the kids with me wouldn't hear the same screaming I heard. It was chilling. The irony was, as soon as daylight appeared, we could hear hundreds of children walking and giggling. They had stayed safe for a night and were headed back to their villages.

Our work consisted of helping out at schools, painting murals, playing with kids, and building a kitchen so the children could eat lunch every day, knowing most wouldn't eat dinner. We visited refugee camps and talked with families that had been torn apart by the LRA, Lord's Resistant Army, led by Kony.

There were countless children who were raising children. So many didn't have parents. Kony's army was full of child soldiers. His practice was to invade villages and force the children to kill their parents, to then force them to engage in his horrific war. Many of the children we met had escaped from his horror. Unlike the year before, on this trip there was a language barrier. The children weren't joyful like they were in Kampala. All we saw was fear and terror in their eyes. Our hearts broke with every story.

Knowing I worked with teens in the United States, one night our guide took us to a teen home. This is where I met my spiritual son, Titus. He was young and working his way through college. That evening, I had the opportunity to share stories with Titus. He told me about his passion to work with street kids. I shared with him about a ministry I was involved with in the United States, *Journey to Dream*.[6] He asked a lot of questions about the nonprofit and our programs. His heart was heavy for the teens in Uganda. At the time, I had no idea what a force Titus would become or how much he would come to mean in my life.

Several years after our trip, Titus emailed me. "Auntie Kim," as he called me, "I have opened *Journey to Dream* in Uganda!" No way, I thought. Did they even have nonprofits in Uganda? Sure thing, Titus sent me the official paperwork and shared the incredible work they were doing. It was unbelievable.

It took me a while to get back but in 2013, I took our Texas *Journey to Dream* kids to meet and work with our Uganda *Journey to Dream* team. Again, my heart felt like it was home. In Texas, our team was known for going out to share a message of hope and overcoming with high school students. Titus and his team were doing the same thing in Uganda. This was, by far, one of the neatest experiences of my life. To see our vision and program being implemented halfway across the globe was humbling.

Journey to Dream Uganda is still going strong today. Titus and his team travel all over their region changing lives and sharing Jesus. God willing, Haleigh, Anna and I will return with another team in God's timing. (The sooner the better!)

LESSONS LEARNED

My eyes were *wide* open during our trip to Africa. I learned why God tells us to take care of the least of these, the oppressed, the orphans and the widows. I learned that we can ask God to allow us to see through His eyes and to feel what He feels. Mind blowing.

I could have held orphans for days, weeks probably, well, maybe much longer. They melted into the arms and chest of anyone holding them, pulling in as much love and nurturing as they could. It has to break God's heart. Every baby, every child, deserves to feel loved *every* day. Yet so many don't, even here in the United States.

I think we all felt grateful to live and be raised on Texas soil, to have such privileged lives. Soon after our return home, we began looking for ways to serve people that needed support or help locally. We started a Christmas outreach in our schools and neighborhoods. We babysat once a month for mom's coming out of prison. The funny thing about missions of any kind is that we think we're the ones helping, going above and beyond, but then we're the one that gets blessed.

At one of our Christmas events, I signed up to wash feet. Honestly, I wanted God to stretch me in doing something I was afraid to do. But my fear changed when I met Ramon. Ramon was a big guy, probably 6'1", 200 pounds, who humbly sat down for me to wash his feet, feet that had been mostly bare during the winter. He told me about his tent in the woods, smiling and grateful for the covering. He had the best smile.

Ramon shared how drugs had ravaged his family. He hoped to see them again one day. He didn't have a coat, and the temperature was below freezing. Yet, not once did he complain.

After I prayed with him, he said, "Miss Kim, can I pray for you?" "I would love that," I hesitantly answered, a little taken aback. Ramon prayed like he knew me, like he knew every detail of my shattered heart. He prayed for favor and blessings, for my children and their futures and for our protection. Jesus was right there with us; I could feel Him. I have never forgotten Ramon's face. I have prayed over the years that he found his way back to his family and somehow made it off the streets.

The lesson here, get out of your comfort zone and do the charity or volunteer work you've been meaning to do. Trust your passion and start simple. If God prompts you to say something encouraging to a stranger on the street, *do it*. If He prompts you to check on your neighbor, *do it*. If He tells you to pray with someone, *do it*. There are so many needs out there. If you can include your kids, do it. There is something special about teaching our children to serve.

QUESTIONS TO CONSIDER

- What cause or injustice burns in you? Something you'd do anything to change or rid from society forever?

- When was the last time you volunteered?

- What is God calling you to do? How is He prompting you to step out in faith? Ask God to give you the boldness and courage to take a step of faith in this direction.

- When is the last time you shared a story of something God did in your life with someone that needed to hear it?

CHAPTER SEVEN

Weekend with Jesus

"If you look in the mirror of God's Word and see someone in need of grace, why would you be impatient with others who share that need?"

PAUL DAVID TRIPP

efore leaving for Uganda in 2005, one of my fellow youth leaders at church, Leslie, offered to sponsor me for a three-day, women's weekend. Though I had no idea what the weekend would hold, when she offered such a sweet gesture, I was all for growing closer to God.

That is, before my trip to Uganda. I had no idea how exhausted I would be when we returned. I mean, aren't we all ready for our own beds and our own showers after traveling? Spending two weeks on foreign soil without a hot shower, eating strange new food, and often using outhouses with holes in the ground for a bathroom (with what felt like swarms of flies covering you), left us emotionally and mentally drained. I wanted to be in my bed and my shower. I didn't want to *have* to do anything for a few days.

Plus, the idea of spending three more days in an unknown place with a bunch of women I had never met sounded awful. I was absolutely not up for putting on my happy face and people pleasing for three days. I tried to get out of it, but Leslie would have no part of it. She insisted I could go tired and would still get a lot out of the weekend.

She picked me up that afternoon and drove me to the retreat center. You can imagine my horror when we sat down in a room full of strangers and half the room jumped up, stood on their chairs, and started doing what looked and sounded like a crazy chicken dance. I was a bit overwhelmed and certain this weekend was *not* what I needed.

But, to Leslie's credit, it ended up being one of the best weekends of my life. By Sunday, it felt like a retreat with a ton of new friends. The volunteers had served us like crazy, running or skating around throwing candy on our tables as we had discussions, carrying our food to the tables every time we ate, and decorating the entire place with flowers, animal print, and inspiring messages. Our beds were even decorated, and the kitchen was full of treats, coffee, and anything our heart might desire. They thought of everything.

It was a relaxing and energizing three days. It was also life changing.

It wasn't so much life changing because of the way we were served or loved on, although that was like something I had never experienced. It was just another revelation of who God is and His unfathomable love for us. It was revelation that took inner reflection (and a lot of tears) to understand. Before the weekend, I had become a pro at "working" for God. The people pleaser or achiever in me was confident working and doing was the way to God's heart. (Also the way to favor.)

God's grace hadn't really been something I studied or even thought about. My focus when I decided to jump all in with Jesus was on works. Don't get me wrong, I knew it was only through grace that I was saved. I just believed once I was saved that my part of the deal meant doing and serving. It meant not sinning. So, I disciplined myself in the big sins and beat myself up for others. I only listened to Christian music. I didn't miss church, ever. I carved out time every morning for quiet time with Jesus. I served and served and served. I was a doer! A few of my friends and family would smile and say, "radical."

I believed the harder I worked for God, the greater the blessing and favor that were coming. I also believed the more I served, the more I could earn His love. Grace, well, that was a new concept for me. A concept God wanted me to understand fully during this three-day weekend. So was forgiveness.

One evening, the plan was to nail a piece of paper to a cross. Literally nail a piece of paper to a large wooden cross with a hammer. I had never done anything like it. Earlier in the day, Pastor Rod, our leader for the weekend, asked us to write on a small piece of paper anything we could think of that might be keeping us from a deeper relationship with God. I couldn't think of anything. My achiever-addict had been in overdrive. Could God seriously want more out of me than what I was giving? (Oh, the ego.)

As I sat and tried to come up with something, the only thing coming to my mind was "*Me.*" Me? It totally didn't make sense, so I asked God again to show me what was keeping me from entering into a closer relationship with Him. Again, the answer was "*Me. Kim. Myself.*"

Several hours later, it made perfect sense. I had done a lot of work on myself, both emotionally and spiritually. I had even come up with a ridiculously long list of sins I needed to ask forgiveness for. I trusted

He forgave me. Next, I listed people who had hurt me that I needed to forgive. I did. But this night, I realized I had never forgiven myself, and honestly when it occurred to me, it felt impossible. I had caused so much pain to myself, to my kids, and others I loved.

My choices and the shame I carried were part of me.
So much so that they felt comfortable.
Freedom from them felt a little scary.

So, on my piece of paper, I wrote "Me," and that night, I nailed it to the cross. As I got back to my seat after making my way to the large wooden cross, I sobbed. Loudly and uncontrollably. The ugly cry we all prefer to do in private was full out for all to see. As I looked around, there were many women doing the ugly cry. We had put everything into this exercise and years of pain and shame were finally released. I forgave "me." The freedom was powerful. However, I somehow innately knew more sin was ahead of me. The gravity of our humanness struck me. As did our desperate need for God's grace. His forgiveness, and me forgiving myself, was a new part of our relationship. Something I've come to thank Him for daily.

Grace and forgiveness change us.

Freedom looks good on you friend. For most of us *people pleasers,* it's much easier to forgive others than it is to forgive ourselves. God's grace is hard to grasp. But, it's impossible to have a real relationship with God without grace. I think, as women, we're usually caught between two places. Either we think and believe we have to work to earn God's love – or we think our past is too messy, too awful to receive His grace.

Neither are true. God couldn't love you more than He does right now. There is nothing you can do to make Him stop loving you, and there is nothing you need to do to earn His love. I can tell you that the sooner you accept His love, fully with all His grace, the sooner you'll find freedom. Freedom that brings peace and strength and joy. You'll begin to like who you are and even those unlikeable people around you. You'll also settle into the truth that you are enough, exactly as you are.

My entire weekend reminded me of my favorite Bible story. The one about *the* sinful woman. It actually says that in my bible, *The Sinful Woman (Luke 7:36-50)*. I'm quite certain if my story was written in the Bible that would be my subtitle. Just being honest.

If you're not familiar with the story, this woman had a past. A past full of sin. She heard about Jesus and all the miracles and healing he was performing in her town. She heard He was talking about forgiveness, which is why she knew she had to see Him.

He just so happened to be having dinner at the home of a very prominent man in town, a Pharisee, who was a leader of the church. If she could just see Jesus, she thought. Could I be forgiven? Could I be set free from all this shame? It's so heavy, and I'm so tired. Her past overwhelmed her. The people in town reminded her of it and the little value she had because of it.

Somehow, she had to get to Jesus.

In her desperation, she mustered the courage to go see him. She walked into the leader's home in the middle of dinner, *uninvited*. Her self-loathing and regret more than she could stand. She knew the looks she would receive, the snickering from some, the gasps from others; but she walked in anyway. The Pharisee, Simon, recognized her instantly, disgusted he thought to himself, "If this man (Jesus) was truly a prophet, he would know who was touching him, and how sinful she is."

Jesus knew his thoughts and said, "Simon, I have something to tell you." "Tell me, teacher," Simon said.

"Two people owed money to a certain moneylender. One owed him five hundred denarii, and the other fifty. Neither of them had the money to pay him back, so he forgave the debts of both. Now which of them will love him more?" Simon replied, "I suppose the one who had the bigger debt forgiven." "You are correct," Jesus said.

Jesus turned toward the woman, reminding Simon he hadn't provided water for Jesus to wash His feet or even oil for His head. He hadn't given Jesus a kiss as He entered. All customary in that day. Yet this woman had wet His feet with her tears, wiping them with her hair. She had kissed His feet repeatedly and even poured out her best perfume on His feet. Jesus then told Simon and the other guests, "She has loved much, and much has been forgiven." He then looked into her eyes and said, "Go. Your sins are forgiven."

Can you imagine? Y'all, I would be on the floor sobbing. First, I would have fallen on the floor, tears flooding His feet just bringing Him everything I needed forgiveness for. I would give Him my wedding ring, iPhone, and anything else I had of value. (I don't use perfume.) Then, realizing I was free of my past, I would jump up to my feet and give Jesus the biggest, longest bear hug possible. I'm sure crying and telling Him repeatedly how much I love Him the entire time.

Free. Think about it. There's no price we can put on that.

Girls, what do you need to forgive? Have you forgiven yourself fully for your past? Or do you just keep *doing,* working and hoping you'll prove or earn your worth? We can't, *Beloved.* There is so much that happens to us as girls and then as women, some things we could have controlled, a lot we could not. Maybe it has to do with alcohol, or drugs, or promiscuity. An unplanned pregnancy or abortion. Maybe an affair, or getting caught up in something unethical or illegal at work. You've hurt someone intentionally or let them down. Maybe the person you let down is you. Whatever it is, it's time to forgive yourself. It's time to forgive others.

Please don't short yourself on God's grace. He doesn't keep a record of our wrongs. He actually finds joy in giving us His grace. It's important we forgive ourselves, so we can forgive others. Unforgiveness breeds bitterness, and bitterness is not a good look. Bitterness only hurts us. And seriously, have you ever thought a bitter woman was attractive? No. They don't have the glow or light freedom gives. That Jesus glow.

LESSONS LEARNED

I have learned and am constantly reminded there is no such thing as a perfect Christian. There is no perfect Church. There are no perfect ministries. I read something this morning by Bob Goff talking about churches touting the message, "Come as you are." Only, when people do come as they are, we try to fix or change them immediately. Believing if we can just point out their sin, they'll conform. No, they'll leave and not come back.

Love changes people. *Grace* changes people. Judgment does not. We've got to allow people to be themselves long enough to trust us, long enough to find the Jesus we want them to find. It's His love that will heal and set people free.

I said earlier in this book that I am not perfect in or at anything. Parenting, certainly not marriage, and absolutely not at being a Christian. I *adore* Jesus, but I cuss when I'm angry. My voice goes up a few octaves after two glasses of wine. I envy what others have at times, and some days think too highly of myself. Other days, I don't think enough of myself and my attitude shows it. I can be judgmental. I can be harsh. I still try to earn love and approval.

But, God's grace covers me. When I fail, I own it. I've learned there's nothing I can hide from God anyway. What's the point? He sees and knows everything. He knows my thoughts, even the embarrassing ones. I don't pretend He misses when I have a sinful thought or desire. I ask Him to change my thinking or change my desires. He does.

Grace and forgiveness allow you to exhale. You stop trying to measure up, to earn whatever it is you're trying to earn. You stop striving. You breathe deeper and smile more. Women who get grace are gorgeous to me, regardless of anything external they have or don't have. They're simply refreshing to sit with.

We're all going to fall. When we do, we get back up, shake the dust off, and keep going. Keep going. Push through. We remember God's unconditional love and what He says about us.

Forgive them. Forgive yourself. Accept grace.

Now, *exhale.* You look beautiful like that.

QUESTIONS TO CONSIDER

- What is keeping you from a deeper relationship with God?

- Who do you need to forgive?

- Are you living under God's grace or are you trying to earn favor by always doing and working and serving?

Consider blocking a day or two to spend with Jesus. You can go away to do this, or simply find a quiet place free from distractions. This will be one of the most difficult things you've ever done, because everything you've ever "not" done will come up in your mind and you will feel like you need to be doing something. Challenge yourself. Take time – just Jesus and you. Ask for His forgiveness if you need it. Ask Him to help you forgive yourself. You're worthy and deserving.

CHAPTER EIGHT

Captivating

"The king is enthralled by your beauty."

PSALM 45:11

"Captivating."[7] Stasi Eldredge's book rocked my world. I am a sucker for romance and a good love story. I believe most women, even as young *girls*, have a deep need to be romanced. In fact, it's hardwired into us from an early age. Life and experiences may skew our view and even our desires, but we are all born with a need to be loved.

I will go out on a limb and say we even want to feel beautiful, chosen, and cherished. Stasi nailed this truth in "Captivating." As I read her words, I become the little girl she describes twirling around on her coffee table, hoping her dad would be captivated by her beauty. And not just captivated by noticing her, but profess her beauty intentionally and out loud.

Sadly, too many dads don't speak this kind of blessing over their daughters. Instead, they may say things like, "get off the coffee table so you don't ruin your dress" or "get down from there before you fall." He may be afraid she will fall. Maybe he really doesn't want her to ruin the dress. The tragedy is, he misses the magnitude of the moment. He misses the heart cry of his daughter.

"*See me!*" That's what we're saying with every turn. With every twirl, "*See me.*"

I'm not a girlie-girl, but I do love to see little girls wearing tutu's, big jewel-tone necklaces and earrings, sparkling princess crowns, and waving glittery wands. I picture my daughters, and every other little girl, twirling around in her tutu and sparkling crown, hoping, waiting for dad to declare their beauty. To affirm it.

By the time I read Stasi's book, I knew a lot about God's character and my identity in being His child. Because I was learning who I am through the eyes of God, I was thinking, talking and behaving differently. A peaceful calm was starting to embrace me. My striving for love and approval began to slow down. Honestly, I think I was settling into the idea that I truly was fearfully and wonderfully made.

As young girls and even into our adulthood, we have a tendency to equate the character, love, and personality of God with the behaviors we witnessed in our earthly dad. At the very least, I did.

This comparison can be good or bad, depending on the relationship we experienced with our dad. I wholeheartedly believe I trusted God's unconditional love for me because my earthy dad loved me that way. I knew there was nothing I could do that would keep my dad, or even my stepdad, from loving me. Their love made accepting God's unconditional love easier for me.

However, if our dad was cold or unaffectionate, we may see God as aloof and uncaring. If we had an abusive father, we may fear God and see Him as angry. If our dad was absent, emotionally or physically, we might think God is somewhere up there but not really interested in us.

In my singleness I longed to be captivating, always dreaming of a husband. In the middle of my longing, when I was still a broken mess, I met a man who had done more work on himself than I had. Okay, let's just say he was healthy, and I was not. He looked at me one day and said, "Kim, you have this insatiable need to be loved and I can't love you like that. No man can. The *only One* who can love you that way is God."

Whoa! What? Embarrassed and a little offended, his words landed on me like a ton of bricks. He was right. I had been searching my entire life for someone to complete me. Jerry Maguire[8] had nothing on the man who would someday fill my every insatiable need. Years later, I still thank God for that conversation and the brutal honesty that opened my eyes. I immediately returned to counseling and decided to get to know this Man he was talking about. What a gift!

I continue to dream and savor love and romance[9], but when it comes to satisfying my deepest desire for unconditional love and acceptance, that's a need only Jesus can fill.

God is Captivated by You

Are we aware that God goes to unthinkable lengths to show us His love? Think about the most beautiful place in the world. The sunset. The mountains. The ocean. The places that have taken our breath away. God created that beauty for us. In part, I believe, to show us just how captivated we can be by something.

The Bible says God knows every hair on our head, every freckle on our face, our deepest secrets. He knows our thoughts, our goings, and our comings. He knows when we sit down and when we rise. He never takes His eyes off us.[10] *Never.*

He doesn't get tired of our talking or rambling. I mean, can you imagine? I am a talker. A complete rambler. I need more than the standard thousand words a day required by most women. God bears the brunt of most of my word count. And although I envision Him lovingly shaking his head at my ramblings, I know He hears – and cares about - every word. He doesn't get distracted or tired of my talking. That is love, gals!

There's a beautiful part of the book, "Captivating," that helped me picture God's attention and love for me. Put yourself in the story as you read it. I won't do it justice, but it went something like this:

> *Wow…. I've never been to a formal affair like this. I feel*
> *a little out of place, and nervous. The room is beautiful.*
> *Look at all the candles. There's flowers everywhere. I*
> *feel like Cinderella.* You smile and giggle to yourself.
> *I love my hair and makeup. She did an incredible job.*
> *And this jewelry, it's exquisite. I even love my dress! It's*
> *absolutely the most expensive thing I've ever put on. I*
> *feel beautiful. Beautiful.* You sigh a long, overdue sigh.

> You sit quietly, hoping for a glance, a look from someone. *I'd love to dance.* As you scan the room, you stop and lock eyes with the king.

> *Wait, the king is looking at me. Actually, he's staring.*
> *Do I look away? Oh, my stomach, the butterflies. Calm*

down. Take a deep breath and smile. Look like you belong here.

Oh, God, he's walking toward me. What do I do, Lord? He's not taking his eyes off me. The music sounds funny. It's muffled. The room feels like it's standing still. My heart is beating so fast. He's holding out his hand.

Is he asking me to dance?

He is.

Ok. Let's do this.

It's the dance of your lifetime. You don't misstep once. Together you simply glide across the dancefloor. Every eye is on you. You're the envy of the room. And THE King is completely, utterly enthralled with *you*, everything about you.

The king is Jesus. He is the King of all kings. *He* is unashamed and passionate about being captivated by you. When you get this truth, you can't help but change from the inside out, beginning with your heart. The truth of God's captivating love can and will bring you healing and freedom like you've never known. *AND*, if no man on earth ever makes you feel captivated, Jesus will. The Bible says *the King* is enthralled by our beauty.[11] Sit with that for a minute. *The King*. The *God* of the universe. The Maker and Creator of all things. He is enthralled, spellbound, captivated by **you.**

Please don't misunderstand. We still need significant people in our lives to tell us we are pretty or to hold us when life is hard. We are made for human connection, affection and love. The difference is, when God is the One filling our cup, anything someone else offers is like the icing on top.

God is relational. He wants a relationship with us. In the first book of the Bible, Genesis, we learn that God created us in *His* image. We are created to reflect Him. If we long for relationship, for deep conversations, to be fully loved and fully known, we better believe that God does as well.

God created us to fill the very longing *He* has in *His* heart for us. Relationship.

The cool thing is, God doesn't force us to love Him. He is God, and He could, but He doesn't. Isn't that our greatest hope? That someone will love us, free of demand and manipulation, simply because they *see* us. It's called free will. Whether we choose God or not, He loves us the same. That never changes. He wants us to choose Him. He wants our hearts. Our time. Our conversation. But, the choice is ours.

I spend every morning with Jesus, sometimes listening to worship music, sometimes reading the Bible. Sometimes I journal and work through a book or devotional. I enjoy it. I choose it. If I miss my quiet time, I feel it the rest of the day. Chances are so does the rest of my household. In my quiet time, I soak in God's goodness. His truth, and it settles me. He gives me the right perspective to start my day.

Do I have a spiritual revival or mountain top experience every morning? Of course not. There are days I don't sense God's presence at all, and there are days I feel like I'm just going through the motions. But, somehow, every time, I'm filled just by sitting with Him. If I miss my time, my attitude and mood reflect much more of Kim and less of Jesus. I find myself expecting someone else to fill my cup and get easily frustrated when they don't (or can't).

Spending time with Jesus is a spiritual discipline we benefit from, a time when we feed our souls and bless God. Try it. Grab your coffee, go somewhere quiet, and talk to God. He's listening. He's captivated by your desire to be with Him.

LESSONS LEARNED

Captivating – I simply love that word. What woman doesn't want to feel captivating? When I finally realized that God is captivated by me, my life changed. (I know I've used the phrase "my life changed" repeatedly, but that's why I call it my Jesus journey. It's a continual adventure and full of change.)

We are born wanting to be seen. Our hearts desire is for someone to find us beautiful and worthy. Don't most of us want to feel cherished? *God* is the only One who can fill that need and desire within the depth of our heart 24 hours a day, 7 days a week. Another person, even a man, cannot even come close to satisfying that need. To expect another human to fill a void that can only be filled by God is an unfair expectation. An expectation that will never be met.

One of the most heartbreaking things I learned was the extent not loving myself had on my daughters. My striving for attention and affection, especially from men that didn't treat me well, taught them to do the same. It didn't matter that I was saying all the right things, teaching them what they needed to know about people and love, even God. They saw me striving and chasing, which told them to do the same. They mirrored my behaviors more than hearing my words. By not loving myself, not feeling chosen, I created an insecurity they mimicked in their own lives.

It was quite confusing for my daughters. On one hand, they had a mom who seemed to be strong and invincible, who didn't need a man. Then, on the other hand, that same mom was chasing and searching for approval, and success, and love. They never saw me exhale.

Our kids need the gift of a pure self-love. We need to understand our identity in Christ. Do you believe God is who He says He is? Do you believe you are who God says you are? Believing both helps us love and care for ourselves in healthy ways. We need to model, authentically, for our children the self-care and esteem we want them to have. That's the only way they will truly learn to love themselves.

Ask God to show you how captivating you are to Him? Ask God to open the eyes of your children so they can see how captivating they are to Him. So they know they're chosen.

Chosen – In Chapter 1, I shared about my lifetime desire to be chosen. While writing this chapter, I caught the end of a television show where a man was gently trying to reject a young woman who was clearly in love with him. It sounded like the lines most of us have heard, "I care about you, but I'm not in love with you." She smiled with all the dignity she could and got into a limo that would drive her away. A familiar feeling rose up in me. I wanted to change the channel. Just as I started to, big crocodile tears welled up in her eyes. I was drawn to her pain. She just quietly and simply whispered to herself, "It hurts to not be chosen."

> *Sister!* Can you relate? I wanted to scream at the screen and say, "But you *are* chosen!" That feeling... it's so devastating, isn't it? As much as you try to tell yourself there's nothing wrong with you, you wonder, "What didn't he see? What did I not have?" I wish God could just tell us in those moments, "Trust Me. I have something even better planned for you." He does. Trust Him. Ask Him to show you His heart for you. He will.

QUESTIONS TO CONSIDER

- When was the last time you didn't feel chosen? How did it make you feel?

- Do you ever feel like you're striving to be something someone else wants you to be? What does that feel like? It's exhausting, isn't it?

- What are you seeking from a man or partner to make you feel complete? Is it working?

- How do you get your cup filled daily?

Read back through the story in this chapter about the beautiful girl and the King. Put yourself back into the story and allow God's love and acceptance to wash over you as you realize, He is captivated by you! Begin to live in that truth. It's the only one that matters.

CHAPTER NINE

Here for a Reason

"Difficult roads often lead to beautiful destinations."

UNKNOWN

ooks speak to me. Some books simply entertain us, while others change us. Rick Warren's book, "Purpose Driven Life"[12] did just that. It sent me scrambling to find my purpose. Who doesn't, in the deepest part of their heart, hope beyond hope that God can and will use the mess we've made of our lives for some amazing purpose? I sure did.

In the corporate and the nonprofit world, I took several personality tests.[13] StrengthFinders by Gallup is by far my favorite and was the impetus for my recent career change. My top five strengths are strategic, positivity, relational, wooing, and communication. Most pointing to sales, coaching, or public speaking. From an early age, my Daddy Keith told me I should either work in sales or become an attorney. This girl loves to debate.

Although I never lost my love for debate, I landed in sales after college. It was a great career and afforded the girls and me a wonderful life full of fun trips, shopping sprees, and many visits to the nail salon.

From the world's perspective, we were "killing it." In other words, I was seeing a lot of success by most standards. A beautiful home and Mercedes in the driveway is what the world tells us success looks like. But, what does God say? I was about to find out.

Journey to Dream

What does it mean to live out *God's purpose*?

In my orientation class at Bent Tree Bible Fellowship, we learned about spiritual gifts and the importance of serving others. My strongest two gifts were faith and mercy. At the end of the class, we were asked,

"If you could do one thing and know you wouldn't fail, what would you do?"

I didn't hesitate. I knew immediately that I would start a Christian camp for kids. I was shocked how fast my answer spilled out. Prior to this, I thought my purpose was clear. I was supposed to make money and be a good mom. Still, the class made me question if I was doing all God wanted me to do.

I've learned that when we ask questions of God about our purpose, He's faithful in bringing the answers. Often it is by introducing us to others who are to be part of His purpose. After all, Jesus sent the disciples out in twos. Why would I be surprised when He brought someone to accompany me in fulfilling His divine plan and purpose?

I met Kari the summer my ex-husband went to jail. Ironically, her ex-husband was already in jail. We talked for hours at the pool one day as our kids swam. We both had daughters who were in first grade together. You could tell they were crazy about each other. And as we talked, the reasons were clear. They were living parallel lives, so to speak, both missing their dads.

The friendship between Kari and me formed instantly. The more time we spent together, the more we realized how much we had in common. We were both working in the corporate world, but in our personal lives dreamed about an opportunity to help kids. We had no idea what we were being called to, but we both carried a burden for hurting kids, much like our own, who were affected by addiction and loss. This dream became the topic of every conversation. We were consumed with the idea and eventually decided to go the nonprofit route. God led us every step of the way, opening one door after another.

Starting a nonprofit was a long, challenging process that would test our faith and try our perseverance, but it was obvious to both Kari and me that God was opening doors no human could. As we did our due diligence, we found there was a gap in support services for teens. We had discussed our own stories and talked about how different our lives may have been if we had mentors or a positive support group when we were struggling as teens.

Journey to Dream was birthed in 2004. And I do mean birthed. We started small with 25 hurting, wonderful teens in our first school program. Friends came out of the woodwork to help with events and fundraising. Others became part of our Board of Directors. It was somewhere around this time that I started to see the restorative work begin to take place in my life. I'm a strong believer that God redeems the painful things we go through if we let Him.

Did we do everything right? Absolutely not. If our first fundraiser was any indication of the mountain before us, we knew we were in trouble. We raised $13,000, which clearly wasn't enough money for Kari and me, two single moms, to make it, but we persisted, and doors continued to open.

We survived the first few years, but not without a lot of tears, sleepless nights, and questioning God. There were days we wanted to close shop, but there were also countless God moments. Times He showed up and off that made us know we had to keep going. With every one we learned to trust Him more and our faith grew deeper.

EBay and Furniture: Not too long after starting *Journey to Dream*, I came home to the dreaded pink slip on our front door. If I didn't pay our water bill within 48 hours, the water would be shut off. Frantic, I decided to sell some furniture because it was the only thing of value we had, and I could get a quick turnaround on cash. I posted our dining room table and chairs on eBay and prayed for a buyer. I cried that night, telling God I couldn't live this way. The next morning, I woke up to an email from a lady wanting to buy the set.

The super sweet family came to pick up the table and chairs. Their well-mannered sons loaded the table and chairs in the back of a truck. As they walked out the door carrying the last piece, the mom stopped and said, "Can I share something with you?" "Of course," I responded.

I could tell by the look on her face she had something serious to say. She asked, "What is *Journey to Dream*?" She had seen the name in my signature line when we emailed. I briefly described the purpose of the ministry. As I spoke, tears welled in her eyes. She softly said, "I didn't need a dining room table. I went on eBay to look for a small kitchen table and accidentally selected your dining room table. When I went to rescind the bid, I sensed God say, 'Buy the table. It will bless the woman selling it.'" She continued to encourage me by saying that God was for *Journey to Dream*, that *He* would bless our ministry. I hugged her and thanked her. The proceeds were enough to pay our water bill and buy groceries. As I closed the door, I cried. In awe of God.

This was the first of *many* God moments. Almost always, they came in the final hour.

The Gift of Electricity: About a year later, my parents were coming to the apartment for dinner to celebrate Haleigh's birthday. Birthdays are big in our home.

Before picking the girls up from school, the electricity in the apartment went off. Robbing Peter to pay Paul[14] was how we lived, so I knew what had happened. I called the electric company and begged the lady for help. She was kind and wanted to help, but she couldn't because of electric company regulations. Even if I were able to make payment and an order was put in that very moment, it could take 48 hours for a service technician to restore the power.

Devastated, I laid on my bed and sobbed. This could not be happening on Haleigh's birthday. Again, I was pleading with God from a point of hopelessness and frustration. I think I said something like, "I am doing everything you have asked me to do, God. You can't expect us to live like this. How can this be your best for us? If this is what we have to look forward to, I'm out. No more ministry!"

I pulled myself together. Angry at God, I knew I needed to figure out plan B. As soon as my feet hit the floor from my sobbing position on the bed, the electricity came back on. But, how? I called the electric company again. All they could tell me was a mechanic working at our apartment must have accidentally switched our electricity back on. In my heart I knew what happened. God. Showed. Up.

<u>Half A Million Dollars</u>: Another one of the most memorable God moments was when we were starting our Capital Campaign to build a shelter for homeless youth. Being a small, grass roots nonprofit, we knew we didn't have the donor base to raise the million dollars we needed. At Christmas time we had been working hard to engage the community, but were still far from our financial goal. Right before leaving the office one day, we got a call from a private Christian Foundation who had supported us in the past. They told us we had been approved for a grant we applied for, allowing us to hire another staff member. Before we could say "thank you," he said, "And our board also talked about helping with the youth shelter. We would like to provide $500,000 as a matching grant that will run through all of next year."

Y'all, we sat in the floor in tears and disbelief. We had never received a grant this large, nor had we ever been bold enough to ask for one. The real God thing: We found a building that year to renovate that cost $425,000. The amount we raised for the matching grant was $426,000. *Whaaat?* You simply can't make these things up. Again and again, miracle after miracle, doors opened. God provided. In fact, God grew our small grassroots nonprofit into a million-dollar agency.

Truly, only God!

It wasn't easy. Just like He does to us as individuals, God prunes and molds and puts ministries through the fire. There were definitely pruning years and years of conflict – a lot of conflict. There were days I wondered if I was off track and days I wanted to quit. There were days I questioned whether I had heard God correctly and days I whined to Him about being tired or ill-equipped or overwhelmed. But, every time I tried to throw in the towel[15], God threw it right back to me.

That is until late 2018. In the fall I began to feel God might be moving me out of *Journey to Dream*. I couldn't imagine not being part of the ministry that had consumed me for over 15 years. After dismissing it for days, I decided to take a few weeks off work and spend time praying. As 2019 started, I found myself explaining to our board that it was time for me to step down. Walking away was hard. There were weeks of sadness and days I felt totally lost and depressed. I feared I was disappointing God (despite feeling He was telling me it was time to walk away). I wondered if He would use me again.

Journey to Dream had been the greatest ride of my life. Truly, a crazy, amazing adventure with Jesus. I had fallen in love with so many kids and seen God truly transform lives, student after student, teen after teen. Like most folks leading ministries or nonprofits, I struggled with compassion fatigue toward the end. I knew I needed to rest because my passion was lagging, and my bleeding heart felt a bit cold. Things that would normally move me to tears just didn't. And if you missed it, I shed a lot of tears. I knew it was time for a season of rest. I had served in some kind of ministry for almost 20 years. I didn't know what it would feel like to just focus on me and my family.

Honestly, it was wonderful. My kids and my husband, who you will meet in the last chapter, deserved my full attention and heart. God knew we were moving into a season where they would need all of me, not just part of me. In time and with rest, my fire for injustice and hurting people returned. In fact, that in part is why you're reading this book. My heart started to come alive for women. Women like you. Women smack dab in the middle of their pain or shattering season. The single mom not sure she can make it another day, the woman overcoming infidelity in her marriage, and the woman simply feeling depleted and not enough. You are why Beautifully Brokenx3 was born.

This world can be a cruel place. We have to anticipate adversity and tragic situations. We're also wise to look up when we feel inadequate or incapable. God is neither, and He loves to do the impossible through us and for us. Please don't believe for one second that if you've been fired from your job or removed from ministry or relocated to another state that God can't use you. That's a lie. He is searching the earth for women to use. He needs you. We need you and the legacy you're supposed to leave.

One of my most favorite things I've read that Beth Moore wrote was when she talked about her own legacy. It stuck with me, as do most of her writings and sayings. Anyway, she said more than she hoped to be remembered for her teaching or writing, she wanted people to remember that she was, "about God." For too long, I thought my legacy would be *Journey to Dream*, and that would have been enough. But when I read her words, I thought, "Me too!" I want my family and friends to say I was crazy in love with Jesus, that I did my best to love like Him.

What if we all tried to live the rest of our lives being *about God*? How different our world might look.

> *Beloved*, God has a divine plan for your life. Even your pain. He will use everything you've ever been through, if you let Him. You are not too far gone. You are not too complicated, too lost, too old, or too whatever. If you're still breathing, God wants to use you. Think about it. There is only one you. There has never been someone with your same passions, your talent or abilities, and certainly not your experiences. He created you for this time in history. Oh, He knew it would be hard. Our planet is in turmoil like we've

never seen before. But *you*, you are needed. Your story of overcoming will help another woman experiencing the exact pain and challenge you went through have hope. She will find the strength to fight and overcome, because you did.

LESSONS LEARNED

Not only is "The Purpose Driven Life" by Rick Warren one of the bestselling books of all time, it is groundbreaking.[16] If you have wondered why things happened in your life or why you're passionate about certain things, this book just might have the answer. It did for me.

The lessons learned during my time founding and growing *Journey to Dream* are far too many to repeat here. I learned what it means to be on an adventure with Jesus. I learned to trust Him and to persevere. To keep the faith when everyone is telling you it won't work. To fight for what God puts on your heart. I learned the thrill of being in the battle and on the frontline.

I think what I learned most is that when we identify our gifts and strengths, when we spend time figuring out how God wired us, it is easy to see where we fit and what we should be doing. We are all so unique. Our differences make it possible to reach the world. Thank goodness we're all not passionate about homelessness. Who would rescue trafficking victims or find homes for abused dogs? Who would grow our museums and parks for people to enjoy and learn?

I don't know if this will help, but here is the acronym used in Purpose Driven Life.

- S – Spiritual Gifts
- H – Heart
- A – Abilities
- P – Personality
- E - Experiences

S – Spiritual Gifts:

Spiritual gifts are an anointing God gives each of us through the Holy Spirit. They are used to support and build the church, as well as encourage and help people. They include things like: mercy, faith, leadership, teaching, administration, encouragement, intersession (strong prayer warriors). My gift of mercy lends well to caring for people that are hurting or sick.

H – Heart:

What do you love? What are you passionate about? What breaks your heart when you see it on the news? Something you want to eradicate or fix? Maybe it's helping victims of domestic violence. Maybe its improving education or helping people get physically fit. My heart and passion is for people who are being oppressed or deserve justice.

A – Abilities:

What are your abilities? What are you skilled at or in what areas have you been trained? What's your vocation or job experience? Are you good at raising money? Have you been trained to help people grieve? My training and sales ability helped me grow *Journey to Dream*.

P – Personality:

What are your personality traits? Are you outgoing? Strong-willed? Organized? A good listener? Energetic? I'm tenacious, so that also helped with starting a nonprofit. I'm also energetic, so hanging out with teenagers was like oxygen for me.

E – Experiences:

What experiences have impacted your life? Both the good and the bad? What have you been through that might help someone else? I struggled as a teen, so I felt I could relate to the pain and issues teenagers face. The challenges I've faced as a woman help me interact with women dealing with infidelity or addiction.

Now What?

Finding your purpose does not mean quitting your job tomorrow nor does it mean going into full-time ministry. You may be called to be in an office, to be a light, to pray with coworkers or encourage people. Perhaps your role is to raise your children in such a way that they have a passion for the mission field or be someone that stands up for kids being bullied at school. Maybe you're being called to volunteer at a local shelter. Maybe you're being called to write a book and tell your story. There are people that need to hear it.

Ask yourself the question that changed my life. What would you do if you knew you couldn't fail?

That dream or desire isn't in your heart by mistake. If your answer is kingdom oriented, get on your knees and pray for God's wisdom and guidance. His answer may not look like the dream in your mind; but trust that God will bring you into His perfect plan.

You're here for a reason! If you're still breathing, He has work for you. Not to earn His love or forgiveness, remember that's where grace kicks in. He loves you regardless of what you do for *Him*. But know, when we serve others, we find joy, happiness, purpose, and abundant life. Honestly, it can be the ride of your life.

Believe it and take time to figure it out.

QUESTIONS TO CONSIDER

- What is your SHAPE? Write it out.

- What is the legacy you want to leave? What do you want to be remembered for?

- What dreams has God put on your heart? What would you do if you knew you couldn't fail?

- How do you feel God may be urging you to step out of the boat[17] and trust Him?

CHAPTER TEN

My SuperPower

"For I will be a fire all around her, and I will be the glory in her midst."
ZECHARIAH 2:5

I don't remember hearing about the Holy Spirit growing up or even in my young adult life. I'm sure I did, but I don't remember. For my first thirty-plus years, I was on "rocky soil."[18] I had obviously heard the term "Father, Son, and Holy Ghost." I think I probably thought it was a Catholic thing. You know, when they make a cross on their chest or in the air. We didn't do that in the churches I went to.

Stay with me on this topic. I know if this is unfamiliar territory, it can sound mystical. I promise it's not. And let me just state again, I am *not* a theologian. Not in any way, shape or form. I'm a flawed human, sharing my Jesus journey in hopes it will help you overcome or press through challenges that may be tripping you up.

Let me try to explain how the Holy Spirit has worked in my life. Jesus taught His disciples that after He returned to heaven, God would send His Spirit. The Holy Spirit. A counselor of sorts. In the Old Testament,

Isaiah predicted Jesus would be our Wonderful Counselor, Mighty God, Everlasting Father, and Prince of Peace.[19]

For a while, I compared the Holy Spirit to my conscience or gut. I've always believed gut instincts were important. *Listen to your gut*, right? While I didn't know about the Holy Spirit in my developmental years, I do remember distinctly feeling a greater sense of conviction after being saved, when it came to right and wrong.

The Holy Spirit is so much more than our counselor or conscience. He is literally God's power living inside us. He gives us the ability to walk away from sin and do things we never imagined we could. He gives us words when we can't find any. He gives us strength and courage and peace - the kind of peace the world can't provide, much more than a temporary bubble bath. He gives us joy. The Holy Spirit is a gift given to us when we invite Jesus into our hearts.

Flesh Patterns

The greatest lesson I learned about the Holy Spirit is when Pastor Pete preached about flesh patterns. Living in our "flesh" essentially means trying to do things in our own strength or giving in to sinful desires. Let me give you some of the examples he gave us that Sunday.

- There is the performance flesh. We see this in folks who seem well-adjusted, outgoing, capable, maybe type "A" personalities who are always busy, striving, and working. In their flesh, they want recognition.
- There is the religious flesh, which shows up as super-spiritual. People who are usually considered sweet or obedient. Their motto tends to be, "What would Jesus do?" And yes, my entire

family turned and smiled at me as Pete described this type of flesh.

- Comfort flesh is shown in people who seem to be easy-going, cautious, and who hate conflict. You might hear them say, "That's not my job or concern." They want to keep the peace at all costs.

- Folks with victim flesh tend to be self-deprecating and complainers. They have a negative outlook. "Look what you've done to me" or "Look what they've done to me" comes out of their mouth frequently.

There were a few others Pete mentioned, most characteristics you can guess. Caretaker flesh. The fixer types. Pleaser flesh presents in people who just want to be liked. Indulgent flesh shows up with the folks whose life motto is "If it feels good, do it." The hostile flesh was last. These are the abusive or angry, domineering types whose motto is, "Do unto others before they do to you." The vengeful types.

Basically, operating in one of these flesh patterns often means hurting other people. It might not be intentional, but the cost can be the same.

The Bible says our flesh looks like sexual immorality or lust, worshipping someone or something other than God. Our flesh breeds things like hostility, fighting, jealousy, fits of anger, selfish ambition, discord, division, envy, drunkenness, wild parties, and etc.,[20] pretty much rebelling against God and the way He tells us to live. The opposite, living in the Spirit, looks like love, joy, peace, patience, kindness, goodness, faithfulness, gentleness, and self-control.[21]

Don't get me wrong – this is *not* about flesh management. That's impossible. We're human, and we're going to sin. We're going to lust. We're going to get jealous, be selfish, etc. The point of this chapter is that God gave us *His* Spirit, the *Holy Spirit*, to do in and through us what we aren't capable of doing on our own. It's not obedience as much as it is deliberately choosing to live, and talk, and be, and love through God's Spirit – or instead, letting *Him* live, talk, be, and love through us. Who better, right?

Below are two scenarios like the ones Pete gave that might help this make more sense: It's easier to understand when you put yourself into these situations:

> *Scenario One:* I'm at a bar I shouldn't be at and see someone I used to date. The indulgent flesh immediately kicks in, "Oh, just have a shot and loosen up a little. A drink will take the edge off. Plus there's nothing wrong with getting my needs met. Who's going to know anyway?" The Holy Spirit tells me (in my "gut") this is not a good idea. He may actually be screaming, *"Run!"* People will get hurt. I *choose* to pray in that moment. Maybe I pray something like, "Holy Spirit, please help me respect myself and (fill in the name). Help me be faithful and walk out of this bar right now." The Holy Spirit will give me the strength and the ability to walk out. The choice is still mine.

> *Scenario Two:* I caught my teenager lying again about drugs. My hostile flesh starts a verbal attack and I hear my own voice telling my child how worthless they are, how disappointed I am. I am steaming. But still, I sense that prompting to do something different, so I pray, "Lord, I don't want to hurt my child. Please reveal what's going on and how to help."

The conversation becomes calm and loving, it is what
my teen needs most at that moment.

At times, I caught myself wanting to please or not confront my
daughters when they were teenagers. I struggled with comfort flesh.
I would rather ignore what was going on than deal with punishing
them or addressing the issue.

Every time I prayed for the Holy Spirit to speak to one of the girls
through me, or even discipline them through me, I was shocked at
how easy it was to do the right thing. The right words just came.

Even today, if I sense my religious flesh (self-righteousness) start to
flare, I pray for God to give me His words of wisdom or to hold my
tongue from speaking foolishness. He does. If I'm having a bad day
and everyone is on my last nerve, I pray for God to love my husband
and kids through me. He does - every time.

I've done a lot of public speaking over the last several years. Whether
I'm speaking to a crowd or a hurting teen, I usually pray that God
will speak through me. Several years ago, our nonprofit was hosting
a sizeable black-tie event. The plans we had for the program and the
entertainment fell through hours before the event.

I panicked initially. I knew I would have to speak and share our story,
hoping folks would be touched and want to give to the organization.
I had no time to prepare, and it seemed every effort I made to create
a quick video presentation failed. Anxious, I went to the ladies room
and prayed. "God, I have nothing. This is totally Your deal. *Journey to
Dream* is Your ministry. You know every heart that's here. You know
every child we need to serve. Please speak through me. Please share
Your heart and Your passion for these kids."

As usual, God showed up. The night and program were a success. There have been many times that I've spoken and my ego got in the way. Trust me, it is never as powerful or impactful as when I let the Holy Spirit speak through me. God not only knows your heart, He knows the heart of the people or person you're speaking to.

When you ask God to do something through you, you may not realize He's showing up in that moment. It's usually after the fact when you see it. Maybe you've been short with your kids and asked God to help you be a better, more present mom. That afternoon, you decide to take a break in your work schedule and go to the park with the kids. You laugh together and tell them how amazing they are, only later to realize it was God showing up through you. Maybe your marriage is on shaky ground. You're arguing constantly. You ask God to be the wife your husband needs. That night, instead of getting angry when your husband hurts your feelings, you hold your tongue. You're both a little shocked, but something begins to change for both of you.

Don't be confused - The Holy Spirit is not a genie in a bottle. But calling on the Holy Spirit for help or counsel, wisdom or peace, is partnering with God. It makes us better people. And don't think for a minute that God doesn't love when we seek His help. He knows how hard this life can be, how challenging relationships are. We're human, but we have a God who loves relationship. A Father who wants the absolute best for us. There is no better Super Hero, nor is there a better SuperPower.

LESSONS LEARNED

I thought for years my SuperPower was saving or fixing people. Actually, I believed if I could just love them enough, they would change and become the person I just knew they were meant to be. Yep, it's like playing God and a gross form of martyrdom. My version of martyrdom was called codependency, and it is **not** pretty once you see it in yourself. In my recovery process, trying to stop the insane cycle of codependency, I found two sayings to be true. One, "where there's an addict, there's always a co-addict." And two, "if you grow up around addiction, odds are you will either become one (an addict) or marry one."

If you're wondering if you too might struggle with codependency, see if any of these statements ring true for you.

- I need the approval of my partner/parent to feel worthy or valued.
- I'm easily affected or controlled by other people's moods or emotions.
- I tend to end up with people who need to be rescued.
- I feel responsible for what my partner/parent does or says.
- I feel like I bend over backwards to keep the peace.
- I have a hard time being alone.
- I have a real fear of abandonment.
- I often doubt myself and my decisions, needing affirmation.

If this sounds like you, you may suffer from codependent tendencies. Sometimes codependency looks like manipulation or like I mentioned several times, martyrdom. Can you see why I said it's not a good look? Codependency often looks like getting into unhealthy relationships with people who "need" us. It may look like constantly seeking outside ourselves for happiness, or even engaging in compulsive behavior to avoid our feelings of emptiness. We may use relationships to fill a void or a need to feel loved and wanted. The kicker is, it's rarely love, and it's not the need to be loved that's the problem.

The problem is our inability to genuinely love ourselves.

Do you see the common thread? It's never an outside job. Another person cannot make you happy, nor should you expect them to. They cannot determine your worth or value. You cannot rescue them anymore than you can turn water into wine. Only Jesus can do that. Don't look at people as projects. Don't let others treat you like a project. Focus on you and becoming all you were created to be. Give *them* to Jesus.

Recovery looks like trusting your intuition, your gut. It means communicating your most uncomfortable feelings and being able to state your needs without feeling guilty. It means finding out what makes you happy – and doing it. It means changing your *stinkin' thinkin'.* Stop taking everything so personal. Set healthy boundaries and bottom lines. Go to counseling. It is not selfish to take care of yourself. Self-care allows you to love others well, not from a needy or demanding place.

And please remember, self-care is more than pampering yourself. Pampering is great. Go get the massage or pedicure, but you must do what it takes to stay healthy. Drink lots of water. Get some sunshine. Move your body. Try mindfulness. Get a good night's sleep. Invest in a hobby. Do *you*. Be *you* for you. I promise you'll be a better wife, mom, co-worker, boss, whatever you need to be.

And again, *you're worth it.*

- Do you struggle with codependency? What can you start working on today to focus on *you*?

- How about flesh patterns? Did you see yourself in any of the ones mentioned in this chapter? What can you ask God to do through you?

- Where do you get your strength from in a crisis or when you're too tired, scared, or stressed to do what you know you need to do? Is it a never-ending source? Reliable?

Ask God to show you the difference the Holy Spirit can make in your everyday life. Stop trying to do it all on your own!

Also, at the back of this book there is a Resource section. I have put some great resources for recovery and codependency there.

CHAPTER ELEVEN

Cowboy Take Me Away

"He has made everything beautiful in its time."

ECCLESIASTES 3:11

Today, I'm sitting in my living room in my favorite spot. I have a big, comfy chair that sits next to our fireplace. Three large windows are positioned on the wall across from me that open up to our pool. It's the most serene place in the house. It's where I have coffee every morning with Jesus before Kyle or the boys wake up. I have thanked God so many times for my life, my family, and this place of retreat. I truly never thought I'd be here.

My journey, I'm sure much like yours, has been a wild one. Full of trials and tragedies. Full of triumph and joy. A lot of joy, actually. But, again, when we're in the pit or we're suffering it feels like we'll be in that place forever. It's hard to think about a rainbow when we're in the middle of the storm. Often, our pain feels undeserving. Life feels unfair. Brutal, like I said before.

But if and when we look for it, good is still there. The rainbow shows up and it's magnificent. I believe there's always a major comeback waiting for us. I mean sure I never got my white picket fence, but man have I been blessed beyond measure. Speaking of blessings, I realize I haven't talked about my husband, Kyle. There's something about saving the best for last. Keeping the anticipation going. Did the princess ever get her prince? Did God bring her that happily ever after? Were the desires of her heart fulfilled? I hear your questions.

My answer would be yes, but not until I finally gave up on my Cinderella fantasies. Although, Kyle would say they linger and, in some ways, I guess they'll be part of me forever. I feel like I did get my prince. He just happens to drive a truck and wear a baseball cap. And, happily ever after, well, I don't look for that until we get to the other side of heaven.

Kyle is *all* kinds of amazing. He is the *best* husband and father a girl could hope for. He is hilarious and literally makes me laugh every day. He's witty, handsome, intelligent, athletic, and hardworking. He's is also 100 percent *man*. Not just a man's man, which he is. He loves to hunt and fish and be with the guys. By 100 percent man, I mean he's not prone to fairytales nor is he into "sappy" holidays like Valentine's Day. Though I do get a beautiful delivery of flowers every February.

He is honest to a fault. Don't ask him if he likes your hair or outfit unless you want the absolute truth. I came home the other day from having my hair cut. The stylist asked if she could curl my hair, and I said, "Sure." I had never had my hair curled with one of those new, fancy curling wands. Remember, I prefer the natural, hippie vibe. Meaning I don't spend a lot of time on my hair. In fact, it's in a messy bun most days. Anyway, not five minutes after I sat down with Kyle in our living room he asked, "So, she curled your hair?" "Yes," I said curiously. He then simply stated, "Please don't do that again."

In his defense, when I went to look in the mirror, my new hairdo had fallen completely flat and looked pressed against my head. I do live in Texas after all, and we usually prefer a little bounce and body to our hair. I even gasped when I saw it. It was a bit dreadful. I smiled and thought about how thankful I am for his honesty. His honesty heals me.

A simple man, Kyle loves me without makeup. He likes my hair in its natural, wavy state. He dislikes when I criticize myself and compliments my voice when I sing. His loving me *exactly* the way God created me has repaired more wounds than I can list. Please don't stay with a man that wants to change you.

Again, he's honest. I never doubt where I stand with my man. He's been true to who he is from the moment I met him. I say all the time that he's good to his core. He's good to me. And to me, he's the most perfect imperfect human I've ever met. He's perfect *for me*.

Kyle and I met in 2016 in a restaurant. In fact, it was a night I was in one of the worst man-hating moods I've possibly ever been in. I was fed up with men, at least on the romantic front. Venting to one of my best friends, Jamie, and vowing once again to steer clear of men, I got up to go to the ladies room and bam, locked eyes with Kyle. He and his friends had been playing golf and were sitting at a table I had to pass by to get to the restrooms.

We did that *longer than a glance*, check-you-out-look a couple of times (I'm known to have a tiny bladder). As silly or as cliché as it sounds, I really did feel my insides flip when we locked eyes. He does have dreamy eyes with long eye lashes, I'll give him that. He asked us to join them. I resisted, yet still, we ended up sitting with him and his friends for a bit. Jamie and I both laughing until our cheeks hurt. The chemistry was obvious. It was one of those magnetic pulls they tell you to run from.

And, I did try to run, girls. He walked me to my car, and as we talked about *Journey to Dream's* upcoming golf tournament, I gave him my business card. (Yes, I know that's not really considered "running.") He was a complete gentleman. I could tell he was different. Still, I was determined not to date him. I even declined an innocent lunch date after church one Sunday. After refusing several opportunities to see him, I finally gave in, and we've been together ever since.

Before I met Kyle, I was sure the infidelity of my past would prevent me from ever trusting a man. But that wasn't true for this man. I trust him. I trust him because he's honest, and like I said, he is good to his core. I can't imagine him ever being mean or saying anything ugly to me. He honors me as a woman and his wife.

I like to say his mom, Gwen, raised him right. She raised him to treat others the way we want to be treated. And when all is said and done, I'm not sure there is a better lesson we can teach our kids than that. Gwen died before I met Kyle. I can't count how many times I've wished I could talk to her – about marriage, her son, and life. Everyone talks about what an incredible person and godly woman she was. I can see that in both her boys.

Kyle's dad, Bob, died the year before we met. The word is Kyle is a carbon copy of Bob, so I know I would have fallen in love with his Dad too. He taught Kyle to have a strong work ethic and what it looks like to be a simple man. He taught him to respect himself and others.

Quiet about his faith, Kyle never tries to stifle the Jesus freak in me – or the dreamer. He lets me be me and all that entails. He laughs when I tell him he's the cowboy I dreamed of all my life. No joke, *Cowboy Take Me Away* was my ringtone when we met. Our boys, Luke and Preston, adore him and think he's not only the strongest man on earth but the funniest and the most fabulous cook. We are without question his priority.

> *Girls,* I share the story of Kyle and me, not to brag, and definitely not to pour salt in your wound or add pain if you're experiencing heartache right now. I share it to give you hope. To tell you God knows your heart. He sees you. He knows what you long for, your deepest desires. He's heard the prayers you've prayed, and even the ones you haven't. He hasn't forgotten you, I promise. He simply wants *His* best for you. And honestly, it's worth the wait.

I believe that God restores what the locusts steal. Maybe you lost your innocence as a child. Your self-esteem as a teen. Maybe like me, parts of your childhood were taken, marriages destroyed, or your dream of white-picket-fences shattered. You've lost battles to addiction or people you loved deeply. You've lost your business, your savings, or your ministry.

**Whether it was Satan or people you trusted
that caused the devastation.
God will restore what you lost.**

Today, as I type, we're in the middle of COVID-19. We went from smooth sailing and enjoying the best economy we've seen in years to all kinds of uncertainty. Will the kids ever go back to school? Will I be wearing this leopard print mask forever? Will my 401K survive? Will my loved ones stay healthy?

Life is hard. It's unpredictable. The minute we think things are going great, the bottom falls out. We're up and then down, high and then low. There seems to be a steady drip of challenges. If there's one thing I'm certain of after 50 plus years on this earth, it's the fact that more storms are coming. I know another shattering could be just around the corner.

What keeps me hopeful and even happy is knowing this life is not all there is. Aren't there times you've asked, "Is this seriously all there is?" By *this*, I mean life? My stepdad taught me early that attitude plays a huge role in the way our lives unfold, but man, even with the best attitude and my prettiest, positive pants on, I still wonder, is *this* it, God?

And the answer is no. This is not all there is. Thank God! Our life on earth is a blip. It is literally a tiny blip of time. Think about it. I mean, think about forever. It's hard, isn't it? Although, God created us as creatures of time, He also designed us for eternity. Sure we choose where we spend it, but the Bible says Jesus is preparing a place for us, a place we can't fathom or imagine. A place with no more sorrow, no more pain, no more disease, and no more death – ever. *Ever.* We suffer so much here. God knows that, and He can't wait to give us heaven.

Sister, I believe my entire journey has been so I could tell you how awesome God is. To remind you that He is faithful. He is trustworthy. He doesn't just sit with us in our suffering, He fully redeems it. He will restore what the locusts stole. I believe with all my heart, He is what we're seeking when we feel lost or empty. He wants us to experience an abundant life, here and now. He wants us to fulfill His plan for our lives in this season, at this time in history.

I can't put into words what God has done for me. This book sheds only a small light on how He's healed me and changed my life. His love transformed me from a fearful, insecure, needy woman to a woman who loves life, has courage, and honestly loves herself. What I've experienced with Jesus is what I pray every single girl and woman reading this experiences.

My hope for you is that if you haven't, you will explore this Jesus thing. He will rock your world and fill every need you've ever had. I hope that if you're exhausted, you rest. If you need a good cry, you cry. It's okay to not be okay. We all have bad days. Sometimes we have bad weeks or even months. I've learned to wallow if I must. To stay home under the covers and watch movies all day if I need. I give myself grace when I snap at my husband or kids, and especially if I drink that third glass of wine or eat half my weight in chocolate. I don't beat myself up if I miss my quiet time or fail to exercise for a week. We're human.

And, maybe that all sounds like a weird way of accomplishing self-care, but knowing what you need and giving yourself the grace to embrace it, is still taking care of yourself. Like I said earlier, identifying and sitting in our pain is an important part of healing. Just don't wallow too long. A bad day doesn't constitute a bad life. Get back up. Find your happy. Get the support and counseling you deserve. And for goodness sake, *stop* the negative self-talk. Slowdown your "yes," and say, "NO." Build healthy habits and positivity into your daily routine. Take care of yourself physically, mentally, emotionally, and spiritually.

Start today if you must. Believe you are worth it. You are enough. You matter. I can't close without telling you that one last time. Your heart is important. Your pain and passion have purpose. Surrender to the fire. *Yes, forging may feel like breaking, but you won't. You'll come forth as gold. You will rise from the ashes.*

Beautiful One, God promises:

"He will give you *a crown of beauty instead of ashes*, the oil of joy instead of mourning, and a garment of praise instead of a spirit of despair." Isaiah 61:3 (emphasis mine)

Now, adjust your crown Beautiful One, and warrior on.

About the Author

Kimberly is a dynamic, high energy speaker who will capture the heart of any audience. Today, she is the founder and president of BeautifullyBrokenx3, a ministry shared with her two adult daughters, Haleigh and Anna MacKenzie.

Together, their stories of tragedy, grit, and grace have inspired a grassroots organization that has been empowering teens to live life on purpose since 2004. Kimberly's success in both the corporate and nonprofit world, combined with her story of heartbreak and comeback, will leave your audience laughing and crying, certain they can overcome and achieve anything. She motivates others to live their best lives and to always dream bigger. As an influencer, she has been able to rally people and communities repeatedly to go big or go home.

Kimberly and her husband, Kyle, live in Plano, Texas and enjoy spending time with their two daughters and two sons.

For Speaking Engagements, contact Kim at:

kim@beautifullybrokenx3.com
www.beautifullybrokenx3.com

About Beautifully Brokenx3

What does the x3 stand for? Well, it represents me, Kim, and my two daughters, Haleigh and Anna MacKenzie. You've already met me and now know more about my life than you could possibly ever want to know. Below is a little bit about us from our site BeautifullyBrokenx3. com. I'm excited for my amazing daughters to introduce themselves to you.

BeautifullyBrokenx3

Beautifully Broken. A PERFECT description of our journey.

I'm Kim and my daughters, Haleigh and Mackenzie, are joining me on this adventure. We expect you're either an overcomer, a survivor, or in the midst of a storm and that's why you've dropped in. If you're looking for connection, you're in the right place. If you're looking for inspiration, we hope you find it. We've had a crazy ride in this thing called life, which honestly doesn't seem to get any less crazy, does it? We're all three doing what we believe we need to do in order to get better at crazy. (Yes, that's a thing.)

Our hope is that you'll read something you can relate to, either in this book or on our website, maybe something that motivates you to keep going, to push through. Or maybe just to give yourself the grace you need. We hope anything good that comes from our trials will assure you that you too can – and will – survive. You will. You can check out our individual bios below. We're a good mix of wanna-be bad asses and princess warrior types who have a little gypsy/boho/glam girl thing going on. We love Jesus and want to make a difference, especially for women experiencing the pit – regardless of why you're there.

We are living proof that God's unbelievable grace and mercy can transform lives. We each have our own stories of redemption, our unique walks with God, and our own methods (for lack of a better word) of recovery that we continue to journey through. We love words and expressing ourselves. We're not experts in anything. We're far from perfect but work every day at being comfortable in our own skin and believe we can all strive to be our best selves every day. That's enough about us. Come by anytime for encouragement, community, and maybe even inspiration. Whether you feel like you're killing it today or can barely get out of bed, we're glad you're here. We get it.

About Kimberly

Hi! So, I'm a mom of many, you could say, but have four beautiful kids in our family: Haleigh, Mackenzie (Anna), Luke, and Preston. I'm married to my best friend, Kyle, who just happens to be the sexiest, funniest, man's-man I've ever met. They are my tribe and my most favorite thing.

ANYTHING you see good in me is definitely because of Jesus. I usually start with that. I am madly, crazy, in love with Him. I grew up wanting to be Jill from Charlie's Angels (or an FBI agent), then an attorney, then a teacher, and well, I somehow ended up with a marketing degree pursuing a career in sales. I ventured off the corporate path in 2004 to start a nonprofit with my best friend, Kari, to help kids devastated by addiction. I'm extremely passionate, a dreamer, a tad sensitive, sometimes loud, and often come without a filter. I love big.

You won't find me pushing a political side. I love my friends regardless of their religion, race, or sexual preference. I advocate for orphans, hurting kids, and well, just about any social injustice. I would spend every summer in Africa if I could. The two weirdest things about me are that I *love* public speaking and I hate shoes.

My story is a mix of beautiful moments and memories with a great deal of tragedy and pain. In my healing journey, I've found such hope and inspiration in books. Books that made me feel less crazy. Books that motivated me to fight for my best self and life. I guess in a nutshell that's my heart, to provide the same kind of space for healing, hope, and inspiration through BeautifullyBrokenx3.

About Haleigh

Hello All! I'm Haleigh. This is my 25th trip around the sun. I live in the beautiful city of Austin, Texas. I guess out of the three of us I would say I am the least attracted to glitter. I have a pretty unique relationship with the man upstairs. I have an out of this world relationship with my dog Blitzen. He is my saving grace and I fully believe he knows it.

I crave music constantly. If I had to listen to one playlist for the rest of my life it would be a pretty colorful one. Consisting of Taking Back Sunday, The Used, Underoath, Paramore, John

Mayer, City and Colour and, of course, The Beatles (I could go on for hours). I thrive off of artistic expression in any form. I'm mesmerized by anything that lives under water. I find joy in flowers, cooking/baking, holidays, children, family, working out, frozen yogurt, *The Office* and the list goes on.

So, if you have made it this far, I hope I didn't completely bore you. My mother and sister are two of the strongest threads that hold this wild heart together. We are all very different. We have pushed through our own storms, but one thing is certain. We acknowledged long ago that imperfection was life, messy is okay and being normal is actually painfully lame. Be nice to yourself today! I'm really glad you're here.

About Anna Mackenzie

I go by Anna or Mackenzie, preferably Mackenzie, which comes with a lengthy background story. I'm 23 years old. I have my own fur baby, Sasha, whom I love and adore and spoil in an out-of-control way. My family is huge, mixed with all kinds of personalities and it has taken years to learn exactly how to love each one of them. Through childhood trauma and, of course, all the drama life brings, I have discovered the biggest blessing. Big families come with enormous amounts of support, love and most importantly, forgiveness.

Not only am I a young adult learning how to create a life I love, I am a woman in recovery from many different traumas and trials. I am a deep empathetic, an artist, I love to love, and I am undoubtedly strong. I am also extremely emotional, I struggle with severe anxiety and depression, dependency issues and, of course,

I'm a 23-year-old-girl, which is one hell of a rollercoaster. I cuss a lot; I am far from perfect.

My amazing mom, Kimberly, and sister, Haleigh, are my rocks. They keep me grounded and have never left me without open arms to run to. We can promise humor, empathy and understanding to whatever it is you are struggling with. I hope you enjoy reading our stories and experiences on our website.

www.beautifullybrokenx3.com

Notes

1 Genesis 50:20

2 Sometimes in life, we innocently participate in things that open spiritual doors for the enemy to step in. As an adult, I know inquiring of the spirits is a sin against God. Satan loves to hook us into thinking he can predict the future, but our future belongs to God alone.

If you have participated in any of these activities: dabbling in fortune telling or conjuring up the dead; witchcraft; Ouija board; seances; psychics, horoscope, horror movies, games that conjure up spirits from the dead, here's a prayer to close any spiritual doors that may have opened as a result of your involvement:

> *Father,* thank you for guiding and protecting me all these years from the spiritual darkness that is always hovering over us, looking for an opportunity to pull us into the pit. I confess, Lord, that I have participated in activities to conjure up demonic spirits in hopes of getting a glimpse or prediction of the future. Please forgive me for stepping into this realm, though unknowing, and going against your best plans for my life. Lord, please close any door that may have been opened because of my participation in this activity. I

bind anything evil that participating in these activities may have brought into my life, in Jesus name, and I loose the spirit of peace and tranquility over my life. Thank you, God, for making me aware of this sin, thank you for your forgiveness and your protection.

³ https://www.hazeldenbettyford.org/treatment/family-children/family-program

⁴ Boundaries with Kids, Dr. Henry Cloud and Dr. John Townsend, © 1998, Zondervan, Grand Rapids

⁵ Boundaries: When to Say Yes, How to Say No to Take Control of Your Life, Dr. Henry Cloud and Dr. John Townsend, © 1992, Zondervan, Grand Rapids

⁶ *Journey to Dream* is a nonprofit my best friend and I started in 2004 to reach hurting teens.

⁷ "Captivating, Unveiling the Mystery of a Woman's Soul," by John and Stasi Eldredge, © 2005, 2010, Thomas Nelson, Nashville

⁸ Flashback to the scene in the movie, Jerry Maguire, when Jerry said to his girlfriend, "You complete me."

⁹ I reserve those thoughts and feelings of love and romance for my husband, Kyle. I will introduce him in the last chapter.

¹⁰ Psalm 139

¹¹ Psalm 45:11

[12] The Purpose Driven Life, What on Earth Am I Here For? © Rick Warren 2002, Zondervan, Grand Rapids

[13] In fact, if you haven't done Gallup's Strength Finders, I highly recommend it.

[14] A phrase used to describe the practice of taking money from one thing to pay on another thing, which often results in the elimination of one debt by incurring another.

[15] To "throw in the towel" means to quit. It's taken from boxing. When a boxer is too hurt to keep fighting, his coach will throw a towel into the ring as a notification that the fight is over.

[16] Dictionary.com defines "mind blowing" as an exclamatory response to surprising or interesting facts or enlightening information.

[17] Matthew 14:22-33. In this passage, Jesus was walking on the water toward the boat his disciples were in. When Peter saw Jesus, he said, "Lord, if it's you, tell me to come to you on the water." "Come," Jesus said. Then Peter got out of the boat, walked on the water and came toward Jesus.

[18] Matthew 13:20

[19] Isaiah 9:6

[20] Galatians 5:19-21

[21] Galatians 5:22-23

[22] John 14:3, Revelation 21:4

Resources

I can't leave you without providing some of the resources that have made a huge difference in my life. Books I've mentioned. Support groups I've visited, and of course a list of Bible verses that remind you of who God says you are.

BOOKS

Breaking Free, Beth Moore
Believing God, Beth Moore
Get Out of that Pit, Beth Moore
(Actually, every book by Beth Moore!)
Captivating, Stasi Eldredge
Wild at Heart, John Eldredge
Purpose Driven Life, Rick Warren
Girl, Wash Your Face, Rachel Hollis
And of course, the Bible

SUPPORT GROUPS

Al-Anon
Al-anon.org
CoDA (Codependents Anonymous)

CoDA.org

COSA (Co-addicts of Sex Addicts)

cosazoomroom.org

AA (Alcoholics Anonymous)

aa.org

Betty Ford (Hazelden) Children's Program

hazeldenbettyford.org/treatment/family-children

Who Does God Say I Am?

Do you know what God says about you? Do you know who God says you are? I highly recommend finding out. These are a few of the verses I love to turn to when I need a reminder:

God says you are:

❖ Chosen.	1 Peter 2:9
❖ His daughter.	Mark 5:34
❖ His beloved.	Song of Songs 6:3
❖ A conqueror.	Romans 8:37
❖ Forgiven.	Acts 2:38
❖ Redeemed.	Galatians 3:13
❖ Delighted in.	Zephaniah 3:17
❖ Free.	Isaiah 61:1
❖ An heir with Christ.	Galatians 3:29
❖ Righteous.	Philippians 3:9
❖ Fearfully and wonderfully made.	Psalm 139:14
❖ God says you are *His*.	1 John 3:1